CW01551422

Little Britain?

Twenty-First Century Strategy for a Middling European Power

By

Julian Lindley-French

Second Edition

Foreword by General Sir David Richards, late Chief of the Defence Staff, British Armed Forces

Little Britain?

"Worn down, doubly decimated, but undisputed masters of the hour, the...nation peered into the future in thankful wonder and haunting dread. Where then was that SECURITY without which all that had been gained seemed valueless, and life itself, even amid the rejoicings of victory, was almost unendurable? The mortal need was Security".

Winston Churchill on the French after World War One (but equally applicable to the British today).[1]

---

[1] Churchill, Winston S. (1948) "The Second World War: The Gathering Storm Vol 6" (London: Houghton: Mifflin)

Little Britain?

Dedication

This book is dedicated to the men and women of Her Majesty's British Armed Forces who serve their country with such distinction as they always have and always will.

Ulysses

"Though much is taken, much abides; and though
We are not now that strength which in old days
Moved earth and heaven; that which we are; we are,
One equal temper of heroic hearts,
Made weak by time and fate, but strong in will
To strive, to seek, to find and not to yield."

Alfred Lord Tennyson

Foreword

General (Retd.) Sir David Richards, late Chief of the British Defence Staff

The British armed forces have been engaged the world over for centuries. In recent years I have had the honour to lead those armed forces in places as challenging and diverse as East Timor, Sierra Leone and Afghanistan. As a soldier leading the army of one of Europe's and the world's leading democracies the importance of national strategy is paramount. In democracies, whilst we may be of influence, it is not soldiers that decide the role of a state in world affairs and rightly so. From my own experience, in spite of the many challenges the British armed forces have faced over the past years trying to bring peace and stability to troubled places, it is Britain's political and strategic standing which is the vital and yet unquantifiable quality that is so often vital to mission success. Britain is no longer a global power but it remains a country held in high regard the world over for the length of its international experience and the strategic wisdom it has gained.

Britain's strategic role has not been without controversy, as evidenced by Prime Minister Cameron expressing deep regret for the massacre of Indian protesters at Amritsar in 1919. However, overall the world can be said to be a better place because of Britain and the role it has played and continues to play.

For the British, national strategy is not something that historically has been designed by committee. Strategy has rather emerged as an evolution of debate between all those charged with great responsibilities, both within the departments of state engaged daily in Britain's foreign and security policy and those without. In the past the ability to make sound strategic judgements seemed to be part of Whitehall's DNA and thus not in need of formulation or categorisation. This was partly a reflection of Britain's genuine power in the world and London's ability to influence events. After all, the truly powerful are less in need of strategy.

However, as Britain has become more modest in terms of both power and ambition it has had to begin properly considering its vital, essential and general interests and values in a more systematic and dispassionate light. This has meant some tough decisions that, when seen in the light of history, may seem prematurely to signal retreat rather than reflect the strategic realities of an unstable era and the latent influence of a still powerful state. That was certainly the case with the 2010 Strategic Defence and Security Review which had to address difficult questions in an especially testing period.

However, the spirit of Britain's greatness, both past and present, was apparent even in this the toughest of times. All those charged with considering Britain's future strategy do so and did so not in the belief that Britain is about to withdraw from the world but firm in the belief that with the right use of national resources and the immense network of influence Britain enjoys, the country can, and should, continue to play a positive and constructive role the world over.

How Britain plays that role is the purpose of Professor Lindley-French's book. He examines the balance to be struck between the civilian and the military applications of power; how process, diplomacy, force and resource are blended in order to decide appropriate strategies. In reading it I was particularly struck by the centrality he places on Britain's role as a champion of international institutions and the legitimate use of force such memberships confer.

As with most such books I do not agree with all the good professor's prescriptions. Equally, as a valued adviser and loyal friend I know his views always to be worth taking into account. They are born of years of exacting scholarship reinforced by remorseless logic and a rare intuition. I commend this book. It will be of great assistance to those charged with considering the next chapter in Britain's great strategic story.

General (Retd.) Sir David Richards GCB, CBE, DSO
Late Chief of the British Defence Staff, London

Acknowledgments

This book has been long in the making and even longer of thought. It would not have been possible without the support and active help of my friend William Hopkinson who tirelessly reviewed various drafts and patiently pointed out the many flaws. Bill, thank you for your patience and unstinting support as I know there are significant tracts of the book and the arguments herein which you find challenging. However, the book is immeasurably better for your rigour and insights. General (Retd.) Sir David Richards and Professor Paul Cornish have also been invaluable friends in this process. My Dutch wife Corine has also had to put up with (as usual) my muttering out loud over the breakfast and dinner tables as I grapple with the complexity of Britain's strategic challenge. She is as ever a paragon of patience. All arguments, analysis, opinions and flaws in the book are entirely my own responsibility.

JLF, February 2015

Little Britain?

About the Author

Professor Dr Julian Lindley-French was born in 1958 in Sheffield, Yorkshire, England and was educated at University College Oxford, the University of East Anglia and the European University Institute in Florence, Italy. He is Director of Europa Analytica, Senior Fellow at the Institute of Statecraft in London, an Honorary Fellow of the Strategy and Security Institute at the University of Exeter as well as Distinguished Visiting Research Fellow at the National Defense University in Washington DC and Fellow of the Canadian Defence and Foreign Affairs Institute. He is also a member of the Strategic Advisory Panel of the British Chief of the Defence Staff in London, a Visiting Programme Director for Wilton Park, a former member of the Strategic Advisory Group of the Atlantic Council of the United States, as well as a Fellow of Respublica.

Professor Lindley-French was formerly Professor of Military Art and Science and Eisenhower Professor of Defence Strategy at the Netherlands Defence Academy, Special Professor of Strategy at Leiden University and Head of the Commander's Initiative Group (CIG) for NATO's Allied Rapid Reaction Corps (ARRC). A former Associate Fellow of the Royal Institute for International Affairs (Chatham House), he was also Senior Associate Fellow of the Defence Academy of the United Kingdom, and a member of the Academic Advisory Board of the NATO Defence College in Rome, as well as a Fellow of the Austrian Institute for European and Security Policy in Vienna.

He was a Course Director at the Geneva Centre for Security Policy and European Co-Chair of the US-European Working Group on Stabilisation and Reconstruction Missions for CSIS, as well as Project Leader for the Atlantic Council of the United States' *Stratcon 2010* project on the NATO Strategic Concept.

Professor Lindley-French has an extensive, international publishing record over many years. In January 2007 he published a book entitled *"NATO: The Enduring Alliance"* for Routledge. In January

2008 he published *"A Chronology of European Security and Defence 1945-2007"* for Oxford University Press which was nominated for the Duke of Westminster Medal for Military Literature. In April 2010 he published *"A New Alliance for a New Century"* in Washington for the Atlantic Council. In November 2010 he published a new Whitehall Report for RUSI entitled *"Between the Polder and a Hard Place? The Netherlands Armed Forces and Defence Planning Challenges for Smaller European Countries"*. In December 2010 he published *"Britain and France: A Dialogue of Decline?"* for the Royal Institute of International Affairs (Chatham House) and in February 2012 he published the *"Oxford Handbook on War"* with Professor Yves Boyer of the École Polytechnique in Paris. The paperback version of the Handbook was launched in March 2014. In July 2015 he will publish a second edition of his highly successful book *NATO: The Enduring Alliance.* His blog "Lindley-French's Blog Blast" (www.lindleyfrench.blogspot.com) enjoys a high-level, world-wide readership.

Big Britain

"In the nature of the world in which we live we don't want to be at home waiting for the next operation…we need to be engaged in that world in pursuit of the national interest…to revalidate the utility of the Armed Forces to government and the nation."

General Sir Nick Houghton, Chief of the Defence Staff, November 2013

Little Britain

"Unattended, our current course leads to a strategically-incoherent force structure: exquisite equipment, but insufficient resources to man that equipment or train on it. This is what the Americans call the spectre of the hollow force."

General Sir Nick Houghton, Chief of the Defence Staff, December 2013

Introduction

This is a book about Britain's place in the twenty-first century world, the strategic ends, ways and means which London must consider and the role and utility of the British armed forces in the drafting and implementation of British national strategy. The need for such a book is pressing. In a BBC TV interview on January 4, 2015 Prime Minister David Cameron implied that the British defence budget would remain frozen at £33bn per annum. In the same interview the Prime Minister also confirmed that the Royal Navy's two new super aircraft carriers would both be "fully equipped".[2] And yet according to the Institute for Public Policy Research (IPPR) if Chancellor of the Exchequer George Osborne is to realise his aim of generating a budget surplus by financial year 2018-2019 further cuts to the public purse of £54.1bn would need to be made, of which £9.3bn would likely come from the defence budget.[3] David Cameron is more modest but has also suggested that if re-elected up to £25bn of further cuts will be made to the public purse. In that political context the coming Strategic Defence and Security Review (SDSR 2015) could well decide if Britain remains a modest but first rate military power or Belgium with nukes. Therefore, this book considers the strategic and defence choices facing Britain and the consequences of another major cut to Britain's armed forces, and their ability to undertake the future operations that doubtless they will be called upon to deliver.

On July 4, 2014 Her Majesty the Queen officially named the first British super-carrier *HMS Queen Elizabeth* at a dockyard in Rosyth, Scotland. When commissioned the 'QE' at 65,000 tons will be the largest and most powerful warship ever to fly the White Ensign. Her sister ship *HMS Prince of Wales* is currently under construction in the same Scottish yard. In many ways these two ships have become bell-weathers of Britain's strategic ambition and strategic seriousness in a twenty-first century world that Russia's President

---

[2] Interview on the Andrew Marr Show, BBC One, January 5, 2015.
[3] Institute for public Policy Research, "Impact of Autumn Statement 2014 on Departmental Budgets", https://twitter.com/ippr/status/540420928640135168

Putin and the sinister and amorphous ISIS have demonstrated will be big, often bad and quite possibly dangerous.

Given that context there are several reasons for my writing a second, special SDSR 2015 edition of Little Britain? Britain is not a small power, even though its political leaders so often give the impression it is. The May General Election takes place at a strategic tipping point for Britain and SDSR 2015 will and must reflect that. My work as a member of the UK Chief of Defence Staff's Strategic Advisory Panel has convinced me of the need for an accessible book about Britain's strategic choices and the place of the Armed Forces therein that is open to practitioners, scholars and a wider, interested public. Moreover, I have also been contacted by not a few people asking if a print edition would be made available. Finally, I had to prepare the First Edition quickly and there were aspects of the work with which I was not satisfied. Therefore, this edition goes deeper into the strategic environment which Britain must shape, considers far more in the round how Britain can shape that environment, with whom and to what end.

A vital choice to be made concerns the future size and shape of Britain's armed forces. A central premise of this book is that the generation of real British influence, and indeed its intelligent application in Washington, Europe and the world beyond, will rest to a significant extent on the capability and capacity of Britain's world-renowned armed forces. Therefore, capable British armed forces must necessarily be at the core of national strategy if said strategy is to be credible in a rapidly-changing world. Only with a sufficiency of hard power will Britain's soft power influence be properly established on the firm foundations of credibility.

In August 2013 General Sir Nick Houghton, Chief of the British Defence Staff, warned that because of defence cuts Britain needed to "re-calibrate our expectations" about the global role and capacity of British armed forces.[4] He might also have suggested that Britain as

---

[4] "General Sir Nick Houghton, Chief of the Defence Staff, Warns Armed Forces Could Become Cynical and Detached". The Huffington Post, 23 August, 2013 http://www.huffingtonpost.co.uk/2013/08/22/chief-of-the-defence-

a nation needed to recalibrate its expectations and the level of ambition that goes with it. It would be almost comforting to think that any such 'recalibration' would simply be a short-term reflection of the financial challenges the country faces. Certainly, for the foreseeable future British governments will have precious little money to spend.

However, it is not simply money that is at the root of all British 'evils'. Attend any meeting in Whitehall or Westminster and it soon becomes apparent that much of the bureaucratic elite appear to think that their essential task is to manage inevitable decline. Indeed, 'managing decline' has become the ethos of so many British governments and too often simply masks the damaging lack of imagination of a political class and a bureaucratic elite who have for so long seen strategy made elsewhere that they now take decline for granted. It is a consequence of the long and often fruitless search for common ground between the American world-view, the French and German European view, and the lack of a political and bureaucratic consensus about which bits of both to support.

This retreat from big British thinking at the top of Britain's government is reinforced by a now well-established inability of Britain's civil service to implement big action. This failure includes an inability to manage big, complex projects successfully; a refusal by ministers to permit the civil service to think long-term or indeed at all about big policy issues; and the progressive politicisation of the civil service by political parties. All three of these failures have contributed to the demise of Britain's once great civil service, a culture of denial at the top of government and too often a refusal by senior civil servants to tell ministers hard facts when giving guidance. Such failings are now apparent across government, reflective of a Westminster culture that routinely places politics before strategy.

It is not just national strategy that suffers from such failings. In August 2014 John Manzoni, Head of the revealingly-entitled Major Projects Authority, admitted that the British civil service is simply not-equipped to manage complex projects and lacks the big-thinking and effective risk management tools vital to the generation and implementation of strategy.[5] A September 2013 report by the National Audit Office (NAO) highlighted the failure of management that had led to the collapse of a massive IT programme designed to support the new Universal Credit system.[6] The report highlighted a recurring theme in which problems are suppressed or denied by a culture that seeks first and foremost to protect ministers from hard truths, or indeed the consequences of their own political flip-flops. When a problem is finally too great to suppress both ministers and the civil service then conspire either to blame others or claim the problem has been solved only for the truth to emerge long after those responsible have moved on. Be it IT programmes or ordering aircraft-carriers a culture of mediocrity often incompetence has been established at the heart of government that afflicts all aspects of strategy, including security and defence. For a long time Britain's relative power in the world masked such failings, but such sleight of political and bureaucratic hand is no longer possible. Paradoxically, as Britain declines strategy becomes more important not less so and yet those charged with crafting effective strategy seem incapable, thus making decline inevitable.

The motivation for writing this book emerged from the cold realisation that the two essential 'truisms' upon which post-war British national strategy is established are in fact myth. The first myth concerns the so-called 'Special Relationship' with the United States. After over thirteen long years of painful sacrifice in Afghanistan and Iraq my many visits to Washington have demonstrated to me all-too-clearly that Britain's relationship with the Americans is 'special' only in the minds of fifty per cent of London's elite Establishment, mainly those responsible for Britain's

---

[5] See "Modernising the Mandarins" in The Economist, 5 August, 2014 pp 47-48

[6] According to Computer Weekly the IT budget has virtually doubled from £396m to £637m. £34m has been written off with a review conducted to establish whether a further £140m will have any lasting value. See Glick, Bryan "DWP Writes Off Millions of Pounds on Universal Credit IT, Damning NAO Report Reveals". "Computer Weekly", 5 September 2013 http://www.computerweekly.com/new/2240204717/DWP-writes-off-millions-of-pounds-in-universal-credit-IT-damning-NAO-report-reveals

defence.   As one senior American said to me recently the relationship is only special if Britain does not test it.

Yes, Britain's 'Special Relationship' with the United States remains vital, particularly the Intelligence relationship, but London must be as unromantic about the relationship as Washington. Britain's loss of strategic direction has been a long-time in the making. Britain lost the will to think strategically during World War Two when the Americans replaced Britain as THE world power. However, as the conflicts in both Afghanistan and Iraq have demonstrated London's blind obedience to Washington can lead to disastrous consequences for Britain, not least because London's neediness of the Americans has critically undermined Britain's ability to think strategically for itself.

The US has only done Britain any favours when it has been in the American interest, which is perfectly reasonable and sound statecraft. For example, in 1941 Britain agreed Lend Lease with the Americans to fund the fight against Nazi Germany on behalf of the democracies. The last payment Britain made under Lend Lease was 29 December 2006 when the account was finally closed with £45.5 million transferred to the United States.[7] To be fair, Washington wrote off a large amount of the loan in the post-war period as a broke British made it clear London could either keep the lights on in Britain or run what was left of the Empire, but not both. Indeed, the US became increasingly worried that the rapid British de-colonisation of the 1950s was helping to accelerate the spread of communism and in time Washington came to recognise that waning British influence could still act as a useful break on Soviet expansionism. Even today, intelligence co-operation over Islamist terrorism is often 'hampered' by the First Amendment of the US Constitution which prevents any constraint on freedom of speech and religion.

---

[7] Along with the final financial transfer the then Chief Secretary to the Treasury Ed Balls wrote a letter to his American counterpart thanking the US for its wartime support.

When the US moved to end the disastrous 1956 Anglo-French Suez adventure, Britain made a strategic choice that has informed London ever since; never cross the Americans. Suez thus marked the final end of British strategic autonomy. Interestingly, France came to entirely the opposite conclusion and determined never again to be humiliated by the Americans.

The second myth adhered to by the other half of the London elite Establishment is that Britain can be a leader of what European federalists dub the European Project. The Eurozone and the existential crisis it has created demonstrate once and for all the utter impracticality and indeed impossibility of Britain playing such a role. Indeed, to do so would in effect mean the abandonment of Britain's vital and enduring role in Europe – to balance power – and in time Britain joining the Euro. Neither Germany nor France would ever permit a Britain outside the Eurozone to play a leadership role, not least because in reality the EU and the Eurozone is one and the same thing. Moreover, a Britain in the Eurozone would have in any case abandoned all pretence to lead. In other words, unless a profound and very unlikely change takes place in London's relationship with the EU the British will become steadily more marginalised in Europe, handing over an exorbitant amount of national wealth to the EU for little or no influence over it.

In 1973, Britain's further retreat from strategic autonomy accelerated when it joined what was then the European Economic Community (EEC) on very unfavourable terms. To prove its 'Europeanness' London effectively broke its ties with the Commonwealth and at the same time abandoned any pretence to an extra-European role. Since then countless Foreign and Commonwealth Office (FCO) officials (and many others) have built their careers in 'Brussels'. To them, any idea that smacks of British strategic autonomy verges on the heretical, as I saw at close quarters when I worked for the European Union a decade or so ago.

This is a solutions-oriented book. However, the book pulls no punches in its analysis of the failings and failures at the top of British government – the High political and bureaucratic Establishment – which have led to exaggerated decline and loss of

15

British influence. In June 2013 I gave evidence to the House of Commons Defence Committee as it began its investigations into Strategic Defence and Security Review 2015. It was an exchange during those hearings that prompted me to get on and finish this book. At one point I challenged the Committee. It was no good politicians spending months preparing a nice report on how to better organise all aspects of Britain's security and defence effort if they the Westminster politicians a) lacked any idea themselves about Britain's role in the twenty-first century world; b) refused to take ownership of any reforms that could force all-important unity of effort and purpose on a recalcitrant Whitehall; and c) failed the true test of this second Elizabethan age; the re-establishment of a properly-considered British national strategy motivated by a sound understanding of the national interest.

For some it may seem strange to be considering British strategic influence just as Britain begins to emerge from perhaps the worst economic crisis for over a century. Certainly, no-one should be under any illusions about the challenges Britain, its economy and its armed forces face. However, post-crisis Britain will still find itself one of the top ten world economies and top five or six military actors and at a time when America is pivoting away from Europe to Asia-Pacific, and the EU (or more precisely the Eurozone) is about to cast Britain to the outer margins of 'Europe'. Therefore, it is vital London breaks out of decline management and again thinks and acts strategically.

Too strong to hide, too weak to lead Britain's need to wield influence via credible national strategy will increase not decrease, especially as the European Union (EU) loses what way it ever had in the world, and NATO moves to the margins of American political and strategic consciousness.

Therefore, the purpose of this book is threefold: to promote a distinctive British national strategy that exploits the power and influence that contemporary Britain still retains; to help break the endemic culture of declinism and short-termism that infects the High Establishment; and ensure that any such strategy is properly Made in Britain.[8]

16

As New Zealand-born British scientist Sir Ernest Rutherford is reputed to have once said, "Gentlemen, we have run out of money. Now is the time to think". *Little Britain? Twenty-First Century Strategy for a Middling European Power.*

Julian Lindley-French, February 2015

---

[8] Jeremy Paxman in his book, "Friends in High Places: Who Runs Britain" has no doubt who is responsible for Britain's post-war decline. "Britain's indecision over her role in the post-war world, the uncertainties over her relations with Europe, the United States and the Commonwealth, revealed the paralysing tendency of the Establishment to cling to the past. Any analysis of the miserable economic performance of Britain since the war must also lay most of the blame on the prejudices and incompetence of the men in leather chairs in St. James's". Paxman J. (1990) "Friends in High Places: Who Runs Britain". (London: Michael Joseph) p 335.

List of Contents

Foreword
Introduction
Contents
Glossary

1 The SDSR 2015 Challenge

Strategic Shrinkage?
Policy versus Strategy
SDSR 2015 and Power
Britain is still a World Power
Strategic Rock of Ages

2 Decline and Fall?

Decline and Fall
The British Strategic Concept
Balancing Legality, Legitimacy and Leverage
The Absence of Statecraft
British Strategic Renovation

Glossary

ABCA: America, Britain, Canada, Australia
A2/AD: Area Access/Area Denial
ANC: African National Congress
ANA: Afghan National Army
ANSF: Afghan National Security Forces
AQIM: Al Qaeda in the Islamic Maghreb
ARRC: Allied Rapid Reaction Force
BRICS: Brazil, Russia, India, China and South Africa
CASD: Continuously at Sea Deterrent
CEBR: Centre for Economics and Business Research
CFE: Conventional Forces Europe
CJEF: Combined Joint Expeditionary Force
CIA: Central Intelligence Agency
CIG: Commanders Initiative Group
CNN: Cable News Network
COBRA: Cabinet Office Briefing Room A
COIN: Counterinsurgency
CBRN: Chemical, Biological, Radiological, Nuclear
CFSP: Common Foreign and Security Policy
CSBM: Confidence and Security-Building Measures
CSDP: Common Security and Defence Policy
CSIS: Center for Strategic and International Studies
CSR: Comprehensive Spending Review
DE&S: Defence Equipment and Support
DFiD: Department for International Development
DGP: Defence Growth Partnership
DNA: Deoxyribonucleic Acid
DSEI: Defence and Security Equipment International
DSO: Distinguished Service Order
DTIB: Defence and Technological Industrial Base
EADS: European Aerospace and Defence Systems
EBAO: Effects-Based Approach to Operations
ECSC: European Coal and Steel Community
EDA: European Defence Agency
EDC: European Defence Community
EDTIB: European Defence and Technological Industrial Base
EEC: European Economic Community

21

EEZ: Exclusive Economic Zone
ESS: European Security Strategy
EU: European Union
FCO: Foreign and Commonwealth Office
FF2020: Future Force 2020
FOE: Future Operating Environment
FRES: Future Rapid Effects System
FSA: Free Syrian Army
6GW: Sixth Generation Warfare
GCB: Grand Cross of the Order of the Bath
GCHQ: Government Communications Headquarters
GDP: Gross Domestic Product
GOCO : Government-Owned, Contractor Operated
G7/8: Group of Seven/Eight Leading Industrialized Countries
G20: Group of Twenty Leading Countries
HMS: Her Majesty's Ship
HUMINT: Human Intelligence
IJF: Integrated Joint Force
IPPR: Institute for Public Policy Research
ISAF: International Security and Assistance Force
ISIS: Islamic State in Iraq and Syria
ISTAR: Intelligence, Surveillance, Targeting and Reconnaissance
ITARS: International Traffic in Arms Regulations
JEF: Joint Expeditionary Force
JFC: Joint Force Command
JFEO: Joint Forcible Entry Operations
JOC: Joint Operating Concept
JOAC: Joint Operation and Access Concept
JSF: Joint Strike Fighter
MIC: Military Interoperability Council
MoD: Ministry of Defence
MPA: Maritime Patrol Aircraft
NAO: National Audit Office
NPT: Non-Proliferation Treaty
NSA: National Security Agency
NSC: National Security Council
NSRA: National Security Risk Assessment
NSS: National Security Strategy
NST: National Security Tasks

ODA: Overseas Development Agency
OECD: Organization for Economic Co-operation and Development
OSCE: Organization for Security and Co-operation in Europe
PLA: People's Liberation Army
RAF: Royal Air Force
RFTG: Rapid Force Task Group
RUSI: Royal United Services Institute
SCO: Shanghai Co-operation Organization
SDR: Strategic Defence Review
SDSR: Strategic Defence and Security Review
SHAPE: Supreme Headquarters Allied Powers Europe
SIPRI: Stockholm International Peace and Research Institute
SNC: Syrian National Coalition
SOF: Special Operations Forces
STOVL: Short Take-Off and Vertical Landing
UAE: United Arab Emirates
UAV: Unmanned Aerial Vehicle
UCAV: Unmanned Combat Aerial Vehicle
UK: United Kingdom
UOR: Urgent Operational Requirement
UN: United Nations
UNSC: United Nations Security Council
US: United States
USAPSOI: United States Army Peacekeeping and Stability Operations Institute
USIP: United States Institute for Peace
USMC: United States Marine Corps
WEU: Western European Union
WMD: Weapons of Mass Destruction

1.

The SDSR 2015 Challenge

"Allies whose current proportion of GDP spent on defence is below this level (2% GDP) will: halt any decline in defence expenditure; aim to increase defence expenditure in real terms as GDP grows; aim to move towards the 2% guideline within a decade with a view to meeting their NATO Capability Targets".

NATO Wales Summit Declaration, 5 September 2014[9]

Strategic Shrinkage?

The first half of the twenty-first century will be defined by the struggle between liberal states and growing illiberal power – both state and non-state. Britain must be at the forefront of that struggle with appropriately-capable armed forces at the centre of a conscious and considered whole-of-government security and defence effort. The Strategic Defence and Security Review 2015 must reflect both the challenge and the necessary vision and ambition to meet that challenge. The armed forces such a review should move Britain towards would by 2025 be an intelligence-led hub or core force with a centre of gravity towards the high-end of the conflict spectrum. The force would act as a command hub able to lead coalitions of allies and partners on robust operations and act alone on occasions during crises. The force would be centred on a significant number and mix of Special Operations Forces (SOF) and specialised professional forces supported by an appropriate mix of enablers and combat support with a significant surge capability from reserves embedded in British society. The force must also be able to operate to effect across the seven domains of contemporary conflict; air, sea, land, cyber, space, information and knowledge and as such would be as adept at working with civilian as military partners, both across government and beyond.

---

[9]   Wales   Summit   Declaration,   5   September   2014,
www.nato.int/cps/en/natohq/nwews_112517.htm

Britain in 2015 is still capable of generating such a force as one of the world's most powerful countries. According to the *CIA World Factbook*[10] Britain has an economy worth $2.48 trillion serving a population of 63,181,775. France has an economy worth $2.60 trillion serving a population of 65,350,000. Germany, on the other hand, has an economy worth $3.4 trillion serving a population of 80, 399,300. As a comparison, the United States has an economy worth $15.68 trillion serving a population of 316,391,000, whilst China has an economy worth $8.23 trillion serving a population of 1,353,921,000. In terms of purchasing power parity, Britain is the ninth richest country in the world and Europe's second richest after Germany.[11] However, in December 2014 the Centre of Economics and Business Research (CEBR) said that Britain had overtaken France to again become the world's fifth largest economy. Moreover, according to the web-site *Global Firepower,* Britain ranked fifth in global defence spending in 2012, with the US having spent $689.59 billion, China $129.27 billion, Russia $64 billion, France $58.24 billion and Britain $57.87 billion, [12] although SIPRI suggests that by 2014 Britain had slipped to sixth behind the US, China, Russia, Saudi Arabia and France.[13]

However, a rapid shift in the balance of military power away from the West is taking place as illiberal powers achieve power parity and then overtake the military capability of liberal powers. This shift has profound implications for Britain's security and defence and for Britain's all-important alliances. Britain is in rapid relative decline, particularly in the military sphere and SDSR 2015 must confront this dangerous reality if the British armed forces are to be prepared for future challenges. Critically, in spite of the stated ambitions of the September 2014 NATO Wales summit Britain's military alliances are faring little better than Britain itself. Whilst the US spent $715bn on defence in 2010 by 2020 the US will have reduced its defence expenditure to a steady-state $450bn. Moreover, thirteen of

---

[10] Unless otherwise states all facts are taken from the CIA World Factbook 2013.

[11] See "CIA World Factbook 2013", http://www.cia.gov/library/publications/the-world-factbook

[12] See "Defense Spending by Countries" http://www.globalfirepower.com/defense-spending-budget.asp

[13] See "Muscle Memory", The Economist, 14 February, 2014

the top twenty defence cutters between 2012 and 2014 were European members of NATO.[14] Russia aims to invest some several hundreds of billions of dollars by 2022 on new armaments and a more professional military. In spite of oil falling below $50 per barrel in January 2015 the December 2014 re-statement of Russia military strategy confirms that by 2016 Russia will surpass the combined defence expenditure of France and Germany. Indeed, in 2015 20% of all public investment by the Russian state will be in the armed forces. Moreover, Beijing grew the Chinese defence budget by 12.5% in 2014, 12.7% in 2013 and 11.2% in 2012, the latest continuous year-on-year double digit increases in defence expenditure since 1989.

And yet the impression given by Britain's political leaders suggests a determination that Britain should remain a first-rate political and military power. In a speech in the United States on 17 November 2010, former Foreign Secretary William Hague said, "We [the Cameron Government] have a clear long-term vision of Britain as an active global power and the closest ally of the United States. In a networked world the UK is now equipped to play not a shrinking but a growing and increasingly effective role – both in promoting our interests and in helping meet the major world challenges, and so there will be no shrinkage of the UK's global role in the lifetime of this British Government"[15] In fact, Britain has been shrinking-strategically ever since, a retreat from influence made clear by London's complete absence from the February 2015 talks in Minsk that was led by Chancellor Merkel and President Hollande in an effort to bring peace to Ukraine.

Defence reviews are far more of a test of strategic shrinkage than national security strategies. Whilst the latter tend to be wish-lists of interests and values, the former reflect and demand hard strategic and spending choices. SDSR 2010 was notable for its lack of defence strategy. Indeed, it was a spending review in all but name in

---

[14] All the above figures the author's own research.
[15] "International Security in a Networked World", speech by the Rt. Hon. William Hague MP, Secretary of State for Foreign Affairs, 10 November, 2010. https://www.gov.uk/government/speeches/international-security-in-a-networked-world--2

the midst of a deep financial crisis. As such, SDSR 2010 failed to strike that all-important balance between ambition, capability, capacity and investment that is the purpose of such reviews. Now that Britain is slowly emerging from the financial crisis SDSR 2015 should re-establish Britain's defence-strategic fundamental principles, irrespective of whether there is a Conservative, Labour or coalition government in power post-May 2015. In other words, SDSR 2015 will demonstrate whether Britain's leaders are committed to yet more strategic shrinkage, or determined to arrest national strategic decline.

Britain's self-evident strategic shrinkage has been made worse by the ever-growing gap between the oft over-stated ambitions of British political leaders and the serial cuts that have been made to the very tools of influence vital to and implicit in Hague's ambition. Rather, money has been poured into the defensive security services as Britain has shifted from engagement to disengagement and even isolationism, and retreated from considered strategy to a series of tactical responses to humanitarian crises and media campaigns. This retreat into politics at the expense of strategy is a failing that has afflicted all recent governments and critically undermined the credibility of successive national security strategies.

In the absence of a strategy that could inform coherent and consistent policy and spending choices governments have tended to throw money at the challenge of the moment with a focus on inputs rather than outcomes. Thus, there is a very real danger that what should be a vital defence review will be reduced (much like its 2010 predecessor) to a political attempt to square a strategic circle as stated political ambitions bear little relation to the over-stretched, under-funded reality of Britain's armed forces.

Therefore, in considering SDSR 2015 it is also vital to consider the strategic landscape into which Britain is moving. Today's challenges suggest two axes of strategic development: a return to big power geopolitics and the danger posed by super-insurgencies, as demonstrated tragically in the 7 January, 2015 attack on the office of *Charlie Hebdo* in Paris and the emergence of ISIS in northern Iraq and Syria. Therefore, it is clear that Britain has much to do if SDSR

2015 is to help strike a credible balance between protection of society and projection of power to interdict, prevent, punish and prevail with armed forces up to the twenty-first century challenge.

Therefore, SDSR 2015's main mission must be to render the British armed forces once again 'fit for purpose' in that now hackneyed phrase, ensure they are armed with the necessary capabilities and capacities and firmly embed them at the heart of a working whole-of-government concept of security and defence if Britain is to meet successfully the many challenges it must now confront.

Indeed, all of Britain's security and defence planning assumptions are in urgent need of review and SDSR 2015 should be at the forefront of such an effort. At the NATO Wales Summit Prime Minister David Cameron suggested a down-payment on a credible strategic future by committing Britain to spending a minimum 2% GDP on defence - the NATO baseline for minimum defence credibility. At the very least SDSR 2015 must confirm that commitment out to 2020 and beyond.

The United States will remain Britain's most important ally and partner. However, if the Americans are to remain in effect a way for Britain to afford strategic influence and defence relatively cheaply (which is what the relationship has become) then Britain will have to be seen to invest in armed forces capable of upholding the British end of a dynamic bargain. At the NATO Wales Summit Prime Minister Cameron revealed a fundamentally false assumption held by all the European allies, but most notably Britain, that the United States will be strong enough to be everywhere, all of the time in the event of possibly multiple and simultaneous crises and challenges the world over. The relative defence stats suggest not.

The conundrum at the heart of the 'Special Relationship' is apparent from the Military Tasks British forces are expected to fulfil. SDSR 2010 laid out seven Military Tasks for the British armed forces most of which are context specific and imply a close relationship with the Americans and other allies. These Tasks can be thus summarised: defending the UK and its Overseas Territories; providing strategic intelligence; providing nuclear deterrence, supporting civil-emergency organisations in times of crisis; defending British interests by projecting power strategically through expeditionary interventions; providing a defence contribution to British influence; and providing security for stabilisation. If the British armed forces are not able to support US forces facing roughly the same task-set, albeit on a global scale, then the US will not be in a position to properly support the British. If SDSR 2015 does not face squarely America's military challenge Britain's own Military Tasks will be impossible to fulfil.

Yes, the Americans are still the strongest military power on the planet and will remain so for some time. However, some economists believe China will surpass the US economy as early as 2016. Moreover, as indicated above the US armed forces are facing defence *cuts* between now and 2020 greater than the combined defence *expenditure* of ALL the NATO European allies.[16] In other words, the great age of unrivalled American military supremacy is fast coming to an end and Britain needs to face up to that new reality honestly. SDSR 2015 must thus take a robust look at all of Britain's strategic relationships, be it with the Americans or anybody else, if those relationships are to continue to work for Britain, the US, and Britain's many allies and partners.

One thing is clear the 'Special Relationship' will soon cease to be special at all if Britain cuts its armed forces any further. Moreover, relative American military decline and the rapid emergence of illiberal powers and strategic non-state actors will change the very nature and scope of geopolitics and re-define what it will take to defend Britain in the twenty-first century. To re-state, the balance of military power is shifting away from Britain and the West at break-neck speed. It is a reality that cannot simply be politically fudged away.

And yet, if SDSR 2015 is properly conducted the review could set Britain back on the road to sound defence, and the creation of a modest but powerful core/hub force that would enable Britain to play a critical role in reinvigorating the transatlantic security relationship.

---

[16] Author's own research.

Such a force would also help strengthen NATO as part of a twenty-first century power 'contract' that keeps the US strong where it needs to be strong – Eastern Europe, the Middle East and Asia-Pacific. Such effort would demonstrate to the world that whatever adversaries and enemies spend on armed force such expenditures will never outstrip the West and are thus a waste of money. To do that SDSR 2015 will need to look hard at how real efficiencies can be found and new strategic partnerships forged. That vision in turn will require a radical British strategic and force concept, a re-commitment of political will, but above all sustained investment in Britain's armed forces.

Given the strategic environment the bottom-line of SDSR 2015 is this; to remain critically strong in every region the US will need NATO Allies that can be credibly strong in and around Europe as crisis first-responders and that in turn means a strong British military. Succeed and Britain will help NATO reinvent itself as an Alliance, and thus be regenerated in the American political mind. Fail and Britain will simply fade into anachronistic strategic irrelevance and the world will be a very much more dangerous place for that.

Policy versus Strategy

Given the centrality of SDSR 2015 to this book the first duty is to clarify the distinction between policy and strategy, as the balance between the two is central to the thesis herein. Much time was spent considering this dichotomy and many authors consulted with a clear tension evident. With echoes of Clausewitz, Basil Liddell Hart defined strategy as, "The art of distributing and applying military means to fulfil the ends of policy".[17] However, that is too narrow a distinction for the purposes of this book. Colin Gray rightly warns of the danger of disconnect between political and military strategy. "Political Leaders need to assert themselves over the military conduct of war if they are to be certain that war will be waged as

---

[17] "Strategy: The Classic Book of Military Strategy", Liddell-Hart, Basil (1991 ed.) (New York: Meridian)

31

vigorously as policy requires".[18]   However, for that to happen politicians must know what they are talking about and want to lead.

Conversely, Professor Paul Cornish makes the important point that states do not need so much grand strategy as the ability to think grand strategically.[19]   However, there must also be transmission between policy, strategy and effect.   Professor Paul Kennedy captures the challenge succinctly, "...the teaching of grand strategy has, by its very nature, to address strategy and politics from the top. Therefore, what transpires at the middle level, or at the level of practical implementation of those policies, is often taken for granted. Great world leaders order something to be done, and lo, it is accomplished, or lo, it stumbles. We rarely inquire deeply into the mechanics and dynamics of strategic success and failure, yet it is a very important realm of inquiry, though still rather neglected".[20]

Given that challenge, perhaps one of the most succinct definitions of strategy can be found on the website of Portsmouth City Council, home of the Royal Navy; "Policy can be defined as a set of ideas, or a plan of what we should or would do in a particular situation. Strategies are about the way we intend to do things to help achieve our objectives in a planned, coherent and co-ordinated way".[21]

Strategic intention is of course the pre-requisite for sound strategy upon which sound defence is built. Sir Lawrence Freedman, in his 2013 book "Strategy: A History," suggests that strategy "...is the central political art. It is about getting more out of a situation than the starting balance of power would suggest. In other words it is the art of creating power".[22]   Given Britain's betwixt and between strategic position in 2015 that is surely sound advice, because it implies the need for reasoned strategic ambition.   Freedman also asserts an implicit challenge for SDSR 2015 when he suggests,

---

[18] Gray, Colin S. (2005) "Another Bloody Century: Future War" (London: Weidenfeld and Nicholson) p. 363
[19] In conversation with the author.
[20] Kennedy, Paul (2014) "Engineers of Victory" (London: Penguin) p. XVII
[21] See http://www.portsmouth.gov.uk/yourcouncil/our-policies-and-strategies.html
[22] Freedman, Sir Lawrence (2012) "Strategy: A History" (Oxford: Oxford University Press) p.xii

"...strategy remains the best word we have for expressing attempts to think about actions in advance, in light of our goals and our capacities".[23] In that context, William Hopkinson, a former senior British functionary, establishes the relationship between policy and strategy against which SDSR 2015 must be tested. Policy, he suggests, is the defining of objectives ("that which we wish to achieve") with strategy the planning of a coherent way to achieve those objectives.

SDSR 2015 and Power

Policy cannot exist without strategy and neither can exist without a definition of power. The literature has struggled with the idea of power for many years. However, all ideas coalesce more or less around a simple truism; that power is the ability to convince others to do what one wants. As J.K. Galbraith famously said in 1975, "Power is as power does".[24]

Set that definition against the National Security Strategy (NSS 2010) and SDSR 2010 and the problematic at the heart of this book becomes apparent. The two 'strategies' were very much the product of a government that having just come to power in May 2010 realised the extent of the financial crisis which confronted it.[25] In other words, both documents were strong on political and bureaucratic short-termism and immediate 'fixes' and decidedly deficient on strategic ambition or political vision. Unfortunately, the trauma of 2010 has reinforced the idea of Britain in permanent decline; a power with little or no idea of its place in Europe or the wider world. Indeed, for all the dubious nationalist rhetoric politicians often use to mask their collective weakness and cluelessness, Britain today is fast becoming a big country that acts like a little one, removing itself from the business of world power, wracked by self-doubt and locked in self-delusion – *Little Britain*.

---

[23] Ibidem, p. x

[24] Galbraith J.K. (1975) "Money: Where it Came, Where it Went". (New York: Houghton Mifflin)

[25] In a memo dated 6 April, 2010 Liam Byrne the outgoing Labour Chief Secretary to the Treasury wrote to his Coalition successor, "Dear Chief Secretary, I'm afraid there is no money. Kind regards and good luck! Liam".

The essential reason for exaggerated decline is that Britain's elite lack strategic unity of effort and purpose. In a speech in the House of Lords on 7 December, 2014, Archbishop of Canterbury Justin Welby demonstrated the divide within the British High Establishment when he called for SDSR 2015 to include the consideration and possible funding of soft power. "Conflict prevention…," the Archbishop suggested, "…seems quite a good investment. Soft power is far cheaper to exercise than hard power. One day of deploying a battalion will cost more than years of conflict prevention work by NGOs".[26] With all due respect the Archbishop is arguing for a dangerously false and artificial divide between soft and hard power that in reality simply does not exist.

A profound political divide was apparent even amongst those charged with drafting both NSS 2010 and SDSR 2010. One group favoured a more traditional balance of hard power concept at the heart of national strategy. Another group believed that Britain's hard military power had encouraged ill-informed politicians to embroil Britain in dangerous adventures made elsewhere. For this soft power lobby Britain was simply unable to maintain the pretence of world power and should accept its fate as simply another small EU member-state. Worse, the absence of strategic consensus within the Whitehall bureaucratic elite reinforces the Westminster political addiction to short-term prescriptions. What both groups failed to realise is that a modern state such as Britain needs a balance of investments to be made in all forms of influence and power, and that such a balance can only be realised by continuous rigorous review. Such rigour should be at the very heart of SDSR 2015, although experience suggests 'rigour' is only welcome when it supports pre-conceived political requirements – the British curse.

---

[26] Drake, Gavin, The Church Times, 8 December, 2014 "Welby calls for national debate on Britain's overseas vision" www.churchtimes.co.uk/articles/2014/5december/news/uk/welby-calls-for-national-debate-on-britains-overseas-vision

Britain is still a World Power

London's dilemma is that Britain is still a world power even if power is itself a double-edged sword; power imposes responsibilities from which a state cannot hide. Paradoxically, during the Blair years political rhetoric suggested Britain was actually more powerful than it was (Britain punching above its weight). Today, Britain punches decidedly beneath its weight. The swing from Blair's over-optimistic view of Britain's role to today's over-pessimistic and cautious view of Britain's role has put the country in the worst of all strategic situations; attracting responsibility London does not want and threat it will not face. Therefore, Britain must at the very least have a balanced concept of its power if the security of the British state and its citizens is to be assured in a complex environment in which competing state power will remain the main driver of change in the world, but in which terrorism will at the same time pose a threat from within society. British strategy must strike a balance between protection and projection and security and defence.

Furthermore, as Britain is an architect of the contemporary state-centric international system, the meaningful, robust and durable stability of that system should be the necessary goal of British strategy, together with the preservation of Britain as a stable and tolerant society honest to the values that define it. Critically, the institutions of systemic governance that Britain helped pioneer, most notably the UN, but also relevant regional institutions such as NATO and the EU, that are central to British strategy, will also need to be invested with real British power if they are to function in way that is beneficial to the British national interest.

Equally, Britain cannot afford to abandon all and any pretension to unilateral action or lose the ability to lead coalitions of like-minded states. The very international institutions that London deems vital to the effective management of stability and stable change and which are thus central to British strategy are either in need of reform, politically-paralysed or both. Britain's ability to reform these institutions will depend on the level of power – civil and military – Britain can invest in them and SDSR 2015 must be cognisant of that challenge. Indeed, both NSS 2015 and SDSR 2015 must be strong statements of Britain's enduring commitment to institutionalised security.

Strange though it may seem given the financial crisis that has so undermined Britain's strategic ambition it is precisely now when Britain should seek to assert maximum influence over change and SDSR 2015 must reflect such ambition. Therefore, Britain must again aspire to a leadership and influence role. However, for Britain to assert such an influence role will demand of Britain's leaders the policy, strategy, organisation and imagination worthy of such ambition, as well as the political will to seize the moment. Britain's "strikingly modest" contribution to the fight against ISIS and the Ukraine crisis does not augur well for future British strategy or influence.

Harvard University's Professor Joseph Nye described national or grand strategy as the organisation of large means in pursuit of large ends. Clearly, Britain still possesses a significant amount of that most important of strategic commodities - influence. However, influence is as nothing if the ends of British strategy become estranged from the ways and the means. That makes any call for an ambitious British strategy seem, on the face of it, perverse. One can only imagine the tut-tutting and head-scratching response of tired, senior practitioners in a London worn down by political uncertainty, financial constraints and diplomatic and military over-stretch; not-to-mention the eternal bureaucratic infighting that in the absence of firm political leadership is a London today that does not know where Washington ends or Brussels begins. However, it is precisely the danger of this moment and London's loss of strategic direction that makes the call herein for a decidedly British-strategic SDSR 2015 not only necessary but vital.

It is particularly important that London stops seeing the avoidance of conflict as strategy in and of itself, particularly if it means conflict with allies and partners over strategy. As Sir Lawrence Freedman states, "...strategy comes into play where there is actual or potential conflict, when interests collide and forms of resolution are required. This is why strategy is more than a plan. A plan supposes a sequence of events that allows one to move with confidence from one state of affairs to another. Strategy is required when others might frustrate one's plans because they have different and possibly opposing interests and concerns".[27]

Strategic Rock of Ages

Looked at from across the ages the need for British strategy is even more pressing. Britain may indeed have come to the end of an unparalleled strategic adventure which started back in the sixteenth century with John Hawkins' 1598 battle with the Spanish at San Juan de Ulloa.[28] If that is indeed the case, the consequences will be profound and not just for the British. However, if the adventure is to end it is because Britain's political and bureaucratic elite have chosen to end it. The facts of power suggest Britain still has a major role to play internationally and militarily.

There is a strange but compelling symmetry to British history that would suggest that 2015 is but a mere hiatus in Britain's global engagement. The true age of Empire began with the 1607 arrival of English and Dutch settlers in what eventually became the United States. Britain's two hundred year domination of the seas can be dated to the 1713 signing of the Treaty of Utrecht that saw Gibraltar ceded permanently to Britain.[29] In 1815 Britain's supremacy was

---

[27] Freedman, Sir Lawrence, (2013) "Strategy: A History" (Oxford: Oxford University Press) p.xi

[28] In his majestic book on the history of the Royal Navy "To Rule the Waves" Arthur Herman wrote of Hawkins 1568 expedition into the heart of Spanish America, "A crucial moment had arrived in the struggle for global power. A new antagonist was about to enter the fray: England. John Hawkin's experiences over the next twelve days in September 1598 would mark the start of a century-long struggle with Spain for dominion over the New World, and also the start of the Modern British Navy". Herman, Arthur (2004) "To Rule the Waves: How the British Navy Shaped the Modern World", (London: Hodder and Stoughton) p 2.

[29] Given the recent contentions between Britain and Spain over Gibraltar it is worth re-stating Article X of the 1713 Treaty of Utrecht. It states, "The Catholic King does hereby, for himself, his heirs and successors, yield to the Crown of Great Britain the full and entire propriety of the town and castle of Gibraltar, together with the port, fortifications, and forts thereunto belonging; and he gives up the said propriety to be held and enjoyed absolutely with all manner of right for ever, without any exception or impediment whatsoever".

confirmed by Wellington's final victory over Napoleon at Waterloo. In 1914, the First World War broke out and, in spite of victory in 1918 the long slide of decline was set inexorably in place. Will 2015 mark the true end of Britain as a strategic power? The jury is out.

Britain also needs to resolve its relationship with the rest of Europe, which of course is above SDSR 2015's pay-grade. In 1962, US Secretary of State Dean Acheson famously said, "Great Britain has lost an empire, but has yet to find a role".[30] In spite of Britain's retreat from strategic autonomy since then there have been moments when it appeared Britain might be finding just such a role in the EU. However, with David Cameron's January 2013 Bloomsberg speech confirming a possible 2017 'in-out' referendum on Britain's EU membership the question of Britain's role and place not just in Europe, but the wider world, is once again pertinent. It is a question made more pressing by the steady and slow disengagement of the US from NATO and the political and military capability vacuum in European security and defence that Russia's actions in Ukraine have brutally revealed.

Against that backdrop Paul Kennedy frames the SDSR 2015 challenge neatly when he writes of a "common conundrum" of any strategy. "...how does one achieve one's strategic aims when one possesses considerable resources but does not, or at least not yet, have the instruments and organisations at hand?"[31] With the revisionism of President Putin's Russia, the global emergence of China and the challenge posed by the ISIS super-insurgency in the Middle East a new world order is finally becoming apparent and it is not one which Britain would choose. It is 'order' in which the global balance of power will be dictated by states very different to Britain and yet states with a very classical concept of power. Can British national ambition be restored and with it a reasoned balance between national strategy and national resources? Is national ambition even

---

[30] US Secretary of State Dean Acheson made this famous comment in 1962. See Porter Bernard, "The Empire Strikes Back", "History Today", 46 Issue 9 1996 (London: History Today) http://www.historytoday.com/bernard-porter/empire-strikes-back.
[31] Kennedy, Paul (2014) "Engineers of Victory" (London: Penguin) p. XXIV

possible? If so, can a proper relationship be re-established between security and defence policy? These are the questions both NSS 2015 and SDSR 2015 must address but will only do so if from the outset the effort is firmly embedded in strategic realism. Is London any longer capable of meeting such a challenge?

2.

Decline and Fall?

"In the end, more than freedom, they wanted security. They wanted a comfortable life, and they lost it all – security, comfort, and freedom. When the Athenians finally wanted not to give to society but for society to give to them, when the freedom they wished for most was freedom from responsibility, then Athens ceased to be free and was never free again."[32]

Edward Gibbon "Decline and Fall of the Roman Empire"

Decline and Fall?

The world in which Britain must compete is one in which there are powerful, illiberal states emerging the leaders of which are legitimised not by democracy, but by the maintenance of economic growth. It is also a world in which Britain is the proxy target of choice for many charged by extreme belief systems, such as ISIS. Britain must also cope with a world of mass movement of people and in which the technologies of mass destruction are becoming ever more accessible to ever smaller and more dangerous groups some of whom are now present within British society. It is also a Big Data world in which the threat of a crippling cyber-attack grows by the day rendering the need to balance openness with resilience.

Threat is thus fast becoming a nexus between mass disruption and mass destruction with open societies the most vulnerable of targets. In the midst of such dangerous complexity the crafting of British strategy worthy of the name will only be possible through a clear-eyed, elite understanding of the realities that must be confronted, the necessary end-states sought, and the costs and impositions the British people must expect.

In that light strategy for Britain means the making of considered strategic choices. Given the strategic environment and Britain's

---

[32] See http://quotes.liberty-tree.ca/quotes-by/edward+gibbon

enduring interests the ends of British strategy require the exploitation of British means and talents to generate the maximum possible capacity and capability in pursuit of maximum possible influence and effect. Such a goal pre-supposes an overarching British strategic concept as enunciated and elaborated by British security policy.

Capacity and capability should certainly be geared to the ends sought, but that goal in turn must reflect a reasoned balance between effectiveness and economy. One of the many nonsenses of official Britain today is the oft-heard notion that in the absence of overt threat there is nothing to plan for and thus no need for strategy, just applied day-to-day process often masquerading as statecraft. Friction is the stuff of today's world and strategy, i.e. informed choices informed by sound strategic judgement, is more not less important.

Take President Putin's Russia. Rory Stewart, Chairman of the House of Common Defence Select Committee, said in July 2014 that Britain had taken the "eye off the ball" with regard to the threat posed by Russia. In October 2014 Stewart suggested in Parliament that Russia was preparing for a major war by 2018. Such an assertion seems strong to say the least, but given the ambition of Russia's 2010 Defence Modernisation Programme, and cuts to British and other European armed forces, the capacity for Russia to use force will indeed become steadily greater. In other words, British military weakness could help encourage Russian adventurism.

The Economist writes, "According to HIS Jane's, a defence consultancy, by next year Russia's defence spending will have tripled in nominal terms since 2007, and it will be halfway through a ten year, 20 trillion rouble, ($300bn) programme to modernise weapons. New types of missiles, bombers and submarines are being readied for deployment over the next few years. Spending on defence and security is expected to climb by 30% this year and swallow more than a third of the federal budget".[33] Moreover, 30%

---

[33] *The Economist*, "What does Russia Want", 14 February, 2015

of the defence budget is being spent to overhaul Russia's nuclear forces and some 60,000 professional 'contract' soldiers are being recruited each year which now represent some 30% of the force. Although these troops are still well below the capability of Special Forces, such as the GRU Spetsnaz and the elite VDV paratroopers, they are fast catching up.

As Russia's forces modernise they are also becoming more aggressive. In December 2014 two Russian Tu-95 bombers flew down the English Channel with their transponders switched off, causing significant disruption to civilian air traffic. Moreover, both aircraft may have been nuclear-armed. There has also been a 400% increase in intercepts of Russian aircraft since 2013. NATO has made 400 intercepts of Russian aircraft since 2013, with 150 of those intercepts part of Baltic Air Policing. There were 68 'hot' intercepts close to Lithuania's borders alone in 2014. Over the same 2013-2014 period Russia conducted eight large-scale 'snap' exercises, and in December 2014 mobilised 9000 troops in Kaliningrad, the Russian enclave between Poland and the Baltic States. During that one exercise fifty-five ships were deployed together with every single type of aircraft in Russia's inventory.

Within that context the real concern about SDSR 2015, and to which Stewart alludes, is the tendency of Government to consider only the input side of defence strategy, i.e. cost and ignore the outcomes of defence investment, i.e. value in terms of influence, deterrence, defence and effect. Where Stewart is correct is that a refusal to properly analyse strategic events inevitably undermines the quality of the strategic choices that emerge thereafter. Such a failure of analysis happens either because the need for strategy and strategic consistency has been replaced by a series of assumptions that are much closer to the immediate needs of politics and the short-term.

Up to World War Two British strategy traditionally combined a well-honed policy mix of power, pragmatism, national cohesion and power projection. Britain was for a long time a key enabler of sound and balanced strategic engagement, even in the midst of previous domestic crises. The system worked. That British society could still produce the creative strategic talent to prosper in the world of the

43

twenty-first century there can be no doubt. However, to do so Britain's leaders must first break out of London's dangerous short-term mind-set if the country is to again properly conceive sound strategy and policy relevant to the challenges posed by the twenty-first century.

That will not be easy. General Sir Nick Houghton warned in a December 2013 speech of what he called "a creeping aversion to risk in the employment of our [British] armed forces". He said such aversion had "...multiple origins – politics, society, the media and the Armed Forces themselves".[34] With the connivance of a risk-averse political leadership much of British society has been lulled into a strange almost child-like state; at one and the same time uncertain and uneasy and yet in many ways disengaged from their own security. Sadly, in the absence of an elite consensus on strategy there can be no honest debate with the people about the aims, costs and responsibilities of security, which is dangerous in a democracy, particularly so given the many challenges Britain must confront.

Muddling through used to be a metaphor for a kind of implicit British grasp of strategy in which nothing was overtly stated, but much was understood. Today, muddling through looks at best the unsteady journey of British politicians from one headline to another and at worst downright denial about the state of the country and Britain's failing place in the world.

Sound national strategy can only be fashioned via a partnership between government and people. Such a partnership must be informed and with government unwilling or unable to trust the people with the fact and extent of Britain's many challenges that partnership today has weakened to the point of fracture. The result is a dangerous paradox; by attempting to maintain the illusion of security it is only a matter of time before the fact of its absence results in the kind of shock which could see an already frayed

---

[34] "Lecture by General Sir Nick Houghton GCB, CBE, ADC Gen, Chief of the Defence Staff, UK Ministry of Defence", RUSI, 18 December 2013 http://www.rusi.org/events/past/ref:E5284A3D06EFFD

partnership between the political class and the people broken beyond repair.

Security strategy must also assume a degree of social cohesion. However, although the decline in Britain's strategic culture and status began long ago, policies that have encouraged mass immigration, discouraged assimilation, and promoted devolution have combined to undermine the social cohesion upon which any sound national strategy must rest. Sadly, Britain today is a fractured place, full of fractured policy serving a fractured society unsure of what Britain should be, or what Britain stands for. Today the very idea of Britain is up for grabs. And, even though political leaders like to pretend otherwise, Britain's recent foreign interventions have helped to radicalise members of Britain's growing ethnic minority population, in particular younger members of the Muslim communities (one must say 'communities' as the Muslim population of Britain is so diverse), making it harder for Britain to act for fear of reprisal. This is especially so in the age of super-insurgency as evident in the fanatical extremes of ISIS and the role of British *jihadis* in the butchery. Unfortunately, such groups and individuals are now actively influencing British strategy as the distinction between Britain's external and internal security fades.

Equally, it is important to put the threat posed by *jihadism* in perspective for the sake of sound national strategy. The threat of terrorism and so-called 'blow back' is very real and could well lead again to spectacular loss of civilian life on Britain's streets, similar to the January 2015 attack on the offices of *Charlie Hebdo* in Paris, and of course the 7/7 attacks in London. However, terrorism as yet does not pose an existential threat to Britain in the way that the rapid rise in the military capability of illiberal powers could.

According to the *Sunday Times*, by January 2015 some 1000 European Muslim extremists per month were going to Syria to fight with ISIS. In March 2013 some 4000 young people in Britain had been referred to *Channel*, a programme designed to counter extremism. There clearly is a problem and it is a problem further complicated by the refusal of many of those responsible for implementing strategy to act. For example, in the twelve months to

April 2014 councils in some 30 areas across Britain spent £1.7m on measures to combat extremism. This is only 50% of the funds available and only 30% of the money spent the previous year. Moreover, Peter Clarke, a former counter-terrorism chief engaged to write a report on the so-called *Trojan Horse* penetration of Birmingham schools by Islamic extremists, said in January 2015 that of his sixteen recommendations none had been implemented. [35]

And yet, there is no reason why new Britain could not be as strategic as old Britain. Much is made of those relatively few extremists who grab the headlines. And yet the evidence is that the vast majority of new Britons are just as patriotic as old Britons. Indeed, the very diversity of contemporary Britain could and should be a source of strategic depth and strength with the right leadership and vision.

However, for new Britain to remain a strategic power the fracture and political correctness that has so undermined the élite's willingness to enunciate a national interest beyond the most trite must end. Yes, strategy will necessarily have to reflect something more akin to a value-interest – an amalgam of the necessary and the aspirational, as that is the currency of this age. However, both soft and hard power, and the influence it engenders, must still be established on fundamental principles of strategy, including strong and legitimate armed forces.

Critically, if London is to shape the choices of others as it must, a conscious national effort will be needed and that will mean a Britain with the necessary power and influence to be attractive as a partner. The need for partnership is important because Britain will continue to bear a great burden of strategic security responsibility for the foreseeable future - too powerful to hide, and yet too weak to lead – a difficult strategic position for any country to occupy in international relations. London has thus no alternative but to properly re-organise and re-aggregate British influence at home and abroad. This will not be easy as the 2014 Scottish independence referendum and likely further devolution suggests that London's

---

[35] See Cavendish, Camilla "Fanatics Fuelled by Culture of Denial and Appeasement" , Sunday Times, 18, January, 2015

hitherto exclusive control of national strategy could well be challenged.

The British Strategic Concept

A defence review however strategic cannot be fashioned in the absence of sound national strategy itself established on a firm strategic concept. A strategic concept essentially concerns the fashioning of balance between what is vital, what is desired, what can be afforded and what can be accomplished. In determining what is vital Britain must establish criteria for determining just how important particular objectives are – effective prioritisation. Those criteria in turn imply strategic method. If Britain's strategic objective is a secure Britain in a decidedly unsecure world Britain's specific goals may be thus summarised: to help keep America strong where it matters; to render Europe a meaningful and credible actor in and around Europe; to preserve the stability of Britain's immediate neighbourhood; to maintain and develop Britain's traditional relationships, particularly those in the Commonwealth, and to play an important role in the emerging American-centric world-wide web of democracies.

Such a strategy has a lot of moving parts all of which demand a properly functioning National Security Strategy (NSS) under the control of a powerful National Security Council (NSC) chaired by a committed prime minister, properly supported by Whitehall and overseen effectively by powerful and appropriate parliamentary select committees. Such a mechanism could translate and transmit considered high-level political instructions to all national lines of security operations – civil and military. Such a system of strategy would finally enable Britain to plan properly and systematically for strategic influence vital if the security ends stated in the National Security Strategy are ever to be realised.

For too long London has refused to face strategic facts and repeatedly put off hard strategic choices. Influence is the stuff of strategy but Britain cannot be all things to all men (and women) all of the time, which has been the essence of Britain's muddling through since at least 1956. Without a clear conceptual

47

understanding of where best to focus British strategy and resources and how best to distinguish between the broad array of threats, challenges, risks and, indeed opportunities, the British face, planning paralysis will afflict government. 2015 is the moment when muddling through must end and choices made. Wait any longer and Britain will be left in the wake of integrating European structures and pursuing, poodle-like, an increasingly uninterested America. In the absence of true strategy what freedom that still remains for the national determination of policy and strategy will soon be lost.

Nowhere will these choices be more important than defence strategy and SDSR 2015 must also reflect that. Defence strategy bridges the gap between capability, capacity and the investment challenges Britain's armed forces face. However, any reconsideration of defence strategy will require in turn a radical re-consideration of all forms of state power and its application. Indeed, nothing short of the comprehensive and creative application of state power in all its forms will be needed if Britain is to generate affordable security, power and influence, given available resources, across Britain's strategic environment.

Balancing Legality, Legitimacy and Leverage

Even though 2015 is the eight-hundredth anniversary of Magna Carta and the seven-hundredth, and fiftieth anniversary of Simon de Montfort's founding of the Mother of Parliaments, Britain is unlikely to influence by ideas alone. The EU belongs to a statist, centralising Continental European political culture alien to Britain, the US no longer sees strategic value in the fading and not-so Special Relationship beyond, maybe, Britain's talent and capacity for intelligence-gathering and interpretation. Therefore, the only way 2015 Britain can generate influence is to bring real power to problems via a strategy that balances legality and legitimacy with real leverage.

Such strategy will not be easy to realise. Unilateral measures have become alien to the business of British government, not least because there is no longer a corpus of knowledge or policy that could be said to reflect any longer a British concept of strategy. The loss of expertise on Russia is a case in point. London failed to predict Moscow's move into Ukraine because within government there were few if any analytical tools or capabilities focused on Russia's intent or capabilities. This lacuna partly reflects a culture in government that no longer sees unilateralism as possible, preferring instead to espouse a thesis of mutual interdependence that Moscow most decidedly does not share.

Ironically, in centuries past unilateral action was very often the essence of British strategy in the form of considered opportunism. As Britain lost the will to act unilaterally, except in the event of the most extreme of provocations such as the 1982 Falklands War, London retreated into the comforting belief that the purpose of power should be alone to shape institutions and influence the choices of allies. This in turn led to a 'strategic' view that accentuated soft power at the expense of hard power.

Today, Britain is fast losing the ability or the influence to achieve even the limited strategic objective of shaping the action of allies. Action, whether multilateral or unilateral, demands credible and relevant power in all its national forms for only such power enables a state to influence the international system in which it is a principle stakeholder, and deter those who would wish it otherwise – such as Putin's Russia.

Equally, as the United States has discovered since 2001, influence can never simply be a function of power alone, especially in an age in which for liberal democracies international community demands moral legitimacy. The growing challenge from illiberal power in the geopolitical hyper-competition of the twenty-first century the distinction between legality and legitimacy (they are not the same) is important. Indeed, illegality and illegitimacy of action is the flip side of power for those states such as Britain that seek to maintain the liberal post-World War Two Western political settlement. *Machtpolitik* might work for the likes of China and Russia in the short-term, but it is self-evidently self-defeating for the democracies (and possibly over time for China and Russia). Architects are far more constrained by rules than demolition teams.

Throughout the eighteenth and nineteenth centuries and in spite of the odd set-back (the American Revolution), Britain was remarkably successful in strategic terms. And yet the rot began to set in a long-time ago, partly because as Britain's room for strategic manoeuvre began to shrink from the 1880s on there was no concomitant development of statecraft installed at the top of government to offset Britain's relative decline. For example, Sir Max Hastings in his book *Armageddon,* is right to suggest World War One had to be fought to prevent German militarism, itself partly a function of Britain's relative decline. However, statecraft would have recognised the moment as early as 1915 when it became clear that no victory at a reasonable cost would be possible for either side, German war aims had been blunted and yet no negotiated peace was sought.[36] Britain's own war aims were further muddled by the Franco-British Sykes-Picot Accord of May 1916 which committed Britain to over-stretch and embroilment. By 1916 the war had already hollowed out Britain's economic base and yet extensive and additional commitments were sought in the Middle East.[37] Had Britain and Germany reached an accommodation in, say, 1916 then Britain's own decline would have been slowed, assuming of course the clique around the Kaiser would also have been wise enough to practice their own form of statecraft.

A war to the end may have been unavoidable, but in the absence of statecraft London lost the ability to explore alternatives and to adapt to strategic realities. Instead Britain retreated into lazy mantras and utterly miscalculated the cost of victory, much as London has done

---

[36] Hastings writes, "It is incontrovertible that the First World War was a catastrophe for Europe. It remains hard to see, however, by what means its statesmen could have extracted themselves from the struggle once it began, in advance of a decision on the battlefield". Hastings, Max (2013) "Catastrophe: Europe Goes to War 1914", (London: William Collins) p. 546

[37] The Franco-British Sykes-Picot Accord of May 1916 took place with the assent of Imperial Russia and concerned the dismemberment of the Ottoman Empire and the division between France and Britain of Turkish-held Iraq, Lebanon, Palestine and Syria. The decisions taken at that time by London and Paris continue to shape the map of today's Middle East and inform many of its divisions.

today over the EU – membership is good whatever form the EU takes and at whatever the cost. In a sense, Sykes-Picot reflected a strategic habit, the habit of imperial acquisition, rather than considered national strategy. The retreat from, or rather the absence of statecraft, led over time to British decline greater and more rapid than it should otherwise have been because it made inevitable change catastrophic precisely because it had been denied for so long. Today, in the absence of strategy, the habit of decline has replaced the habit of acquisition as national strategy has been replaced by politics, process and the management of decline itself.

Decline management is not without irony because the legitimate influencing of others is what many around the world expect of the British, and still regard as somehow the British strategic genius. Indeed, it was precisely the genius for the successful influencing of others that made Britain a great power over two and a half centuries. A relatively small island-state off the north-west coast of the Euro-Asian landmass was not pre-ordained to lead. However, in the absence of statecraft Britain lacks the vision, skills, freedom but above all the ambition and will to 'parley' what strength Britain still possesses into strategic effect.

Naturally, there is a link between strategy and economy. In the eighteenth century strategy became assumed because power was apparent. Indeed, once a number of valuable colonies had been established and protected and trade developed the Bank of England, allied to Britain's leadership of the Industrial Revolution, led London to assume and expect leadership. And, ultimately, it is the loss of economic power that Britain has found so difficult to manage. Between 1919 and the mid-thirties Britain too often assumed status without power and thus failed to adapt strategy to relative weakness. Post World War Two Britain faced with the loss of empire and status began to exaggerate Britain's power.

Consequently, there is insufficient British grip on the ends, ways and means of strategy, which are the essential foundations upon which successful national strategy is established. The British Empire was rather haphazardly acquired, but once established it was maintained by an almost instinctive understanding of the relationship between

51

the strategically feasible, the politically practicable and the necessary.

Therefore, if sound British strategy is to be re-established it must have purpose, relevance and meaning. Indeed, whilst all strategy is political it must nevertheless be based upon a clear understanding of the consistent national interest by the political leadership. It is that understanding that seems too often to be clouded by short-termism and politicians more interested in the latest political fad, under pressure from this pressure group or that, and clearly unsure of how to lead Britain in a hyper-competitive world. Contemporary British strategy is thus in danger of becoming the very antithesis of strategy – politics. Indeed, the sacrificing of strategy for politics is the scourge of contemporary British leaders for it destroys the ability of political leaders to see the all-important big strategic picture. In such circumstances the machinery of government becomes much more interested in protecting ministers than protecting the country.

For national strategy to function it must be essentially Clausewitzian in character in that a hard understanding of power and influence must be seen as key to the realisation of national ends by all national means.[38] However, in the absence of a big picture the means become the ends. In the past the weight of the military aspects of British strategy overborne what should have been political objectives. Indeed, sound national strategy cannot exist without a consistent political vision towards which it works, whatever constraint and set-backs are encountered on the way. However, in the absence of such a vision the defence budget today is being used as a cash cow to fund ring-fenced areas of government policy, such as international development, education and (of course) the National Health Service.

---

[38] In "On War" Clausewitz wrote under the heading "Ends and Means in Strategy", "Strategy has in the first instance only the victory that is the tactical result, as a means to its object, and ultimately those things that lead to peace. The application of its means to this object is at one and the same time attended by circumstances which have an influence thereon more or less". Rapaport, Anatol (Ed.) (1982 ed.) "Carl von Clausewitz: On War", (London: Penguin Books) p 194.

The essential point of British strategy is the successful shaping of the strategic environment in accordance with British national interests to keep the British people secure and reasonably prosperous: nothing more, nothing less. However, deeds have not kept pace with words with British leaders too often failing to invest sufficient political capital or resources in the ways and means of such a goal as they lurch from one headline to another. This has exacerbated the tendency towards incremental retreat which in turn has rendered Britain vulnerable to the buffeting of events, and further reduced the capacity of British leaders to influence Britain's changing strategic environment. To prevent such buffeting Britain's leaders must re-learn the art of thinking independently and strategically and ensure sound defence policy is again at the heart of national strategy. If not London will continue to build castles in the air until a future shock brings them crashing down.

Action is needed. The British have been rightly suspicious of radical prescriptions for international relations and thus understandably nervous of 'grand' strategies, and 'les grands dessins' that have too often found favour on the other sides of both the Atlantic and the Channel. Indeed, the role of 'balancer', i.e. preventing extreme behaviour by others, is deeply embedded in the British strategic psyche. However, with the creation of the Eurozone Britain's traditional role as Europe's balancer has been effectively blocked by France and Germany. Ironically, Britain's role as balancer is as important to Europe today as it ever was, for behind the Euro-speak about political union and one hundred years on from World War One, the balancing of state power, most notably German state power, is still relevant as is the need to avoid the replacement of democracy by some form of over-mighty Brussels bureaucracy. The question of course is how.

To paraphrase Lord Palmerston's famous dictum that Britain has neither permanent friends nor enemies, only permanent interests Britain today seems to have neither clear enemies nor reliable friends.[39] To compensate for this vacuum and the retreat from

---

[39] Viscount Lord Palmerston is held up as the apotheosis of the British Foreign Secretary at the height of imperial British power. However, his famous dictum

53

strategy it has helped engender London too often appears to see the pursuit of the national interest as a series of transactional trade promotion events. It is as though Britain has retreated into the kind of mercantilism that drove the early British Empire as an alternative to considered national strategy, albeit without any of the self-righteous certainty and self-belief that drove many of the early imperialists. David Cameron's 2014 foray to China smacked all too clearly of a pleading, transactional foreign policy at a time when an assertive and nationalistic China is beginning to extend its strategic fiat across East Asia. Certainly, trade is vital but it would be a profound mistake to believe Britain can assure its security and prosperity by reducing strategy to a series of iterative transactions based on trade alone.

The strength of Britain's partnerships and alliances will, of course, ebb and flow given political and strategic requirements at any given time - that is the nature of international politics. However, too much is invested by government in re-labelling impotence to mask the pace and extent of self-imposed relative decline from the British people, rather than properly investing in the alliances and partnerships necessary for today's world to better prepare Britain for tomorrow's world. It is as though institutions have become ends in and of themselves for Britain, alibis for a retreat from power. However, for the self-same institutions to function in the British interest they must be invested with real British power. The very process of retreat has led to a dangerous conflation in the British elite mind with the belief that what, say, the EU or UN wants is somehow what Britain wants, rather than seeing institutions as the safe arenas for safe competition between states seeking to influence change in their favour.

---

masked a reactive, interventionist policy that lacked either imagination or strategy. Former Foreign Secretary Douglas Hurd writes "Palmerston's crime was not his doctrine of interference, but the thoughtless way in which it was deployed. He made no attempt to combine his sporadic interventions with a longer-term plan". Hurd, Douglas (2010) "Choose Your Weapons: The British Foreign Secretary 200 Years of Argument, Success and Failure. (London: Nicholson and Weidenfeld) p. 114.

The emergence of China, and indeed others (see next chapter) onto the world stage, is leading to a new balance of global power and the return of geopolitics. However, to respond effectively to such change Britain's leaders need to become far more adept at defining Britain's abiding interests and the role of institutions therein in preventing the dangerous excesses of illiberal states.

Indeed, unless London's declinist view of the utility of institutions is overcome decline could well become not just a self-fulfilling prophecy but a fatal self-fulfilling prophecy for the institutions themselves. The zero sum game and with it the idea that if power rises on one part of the planet it must by definition decline elsewhere is a compelling and neat academic treatise. However, there is no automatic reason why an increase in the power of China, Russia, or any other group or state, should automatically lead to a loss of British power IF power as a whole increases. The effective wielding of state power is subject to many factors, including will, intent, capability and experience and there is no reason why a state such as Britain could not again become an effective exponent, and international institutions effective arenas for safe state competition – if Britain invests in them with more than words.

The EU is again a case in point. Britain's marginalisation in 'Europe' is now all too apparent and probably irreversible, even if Britain is one of the natural leaders of Europe's security and defence effort (especially from the perspective of an author who has lived in Continental Europe for the past fifteen years). Stopping that of which Britain does not approve, which has in effect been what passes for a British European policy for many years, hardly constitutes the shaping of Europe's role in the wider world.

Britain's marginalisation in Europe has happened precisely because politicians over several generations have refused to compete in Europe over fundamental issues of political governance, not least the nature of the EU itself – intergovernmental alliance or budding super-state. Rather, London has contrived to ignore or play down the longer-term strategic implications of the EU's growing supranationalism, in favour of limiting any short-term domestic political damage. Quite simply the British elite have got the EU spectacularly wrong because they focussed on the domestic politics of the moment rather than future strategic implications. They failed in 1991 to see the strategic implications of the creation of the single currency with the Treaty of Maastricht. And, in 2007 they completely failed to understand just how much power they were handing over to Brussels with the Treaty of Lisbon. Instead, London clung onto the false belief that the widening of the EU to new members in Central and Eastern Europe would prevent the deepening of European integration and thus the marginalisation of Britain. In fact, most of the new members Britain championed have proven to be enthusiastic believers in the 'ever closer union' that British politicians have spectacularly failed to prevent. Indeed, so incompetent has been Britain's Europe strategy that only by threatening to leave the EU does London now have any hope of preventing the seemingly inexorable march towards some form of hybrid super-state in which most of Europe is 'integrated' around Germany. What if that 'strategy' fails?

If Britain's ability to influence Europe is now effectively blocked Britain must look elsewhere for friends and partners and understand the importance of Britain's armed forces as part of the strategic brand central to Britain's wider influence. This is important because Britain can still be an influential actor, not least because ultimately globalisation will likely trump Europeanisation, as the two dynamics are not just different, but too often flatly opposed. One approach for Britain could be to adopt a much more pro-active approach to shaping the policies of new regional cornerstone powers, such as India, Nigeria and possibly South Africa, with whom Britain shares a heritage, particularly in the military sphere. Implied guilt, real or perceived, on the part of the British about Britain's imperial past has no place in the contemporary pursuit of British interests. There are times when robust strategy is not only required, but essential for achieving national goals and that must not be hampered by misplaced or inappropriate re-interpretations of history.

Again, it is precisely the confusion of values with interests that has done so much to blunt Britain's strategic effectiveness over recent years. Britain must clearly determine its contemporary interests and decide their relative priority and weight and whilst the dissemination

56

of values may well be a material interest, at the very least a method for distinguishing between the two is urgently needed. That in principle should be the purpose of the National Security Strategy.

Strategic schizophrenia at the top has also undermined strategic consistency. Britain has swung between investing political energy in an essentially tactical, iterative attempt to hang onto the American superpower and trying to maintain its leading place within international institutions, without actually investing the political capital or military means necessary to maintain such influence. That is why British 'strategy' has been reduced so often to reacting to the whims of others.

British Strategic Renovation

What is the purpose of British influence? [40] This dilemma generates the confusion of values with interests in London that often lead to policies that on the face of it bear little or no relation to Britain's strategic interests, and most certainly not its defence interests. For example, until 2012 India remained the biggest recipient of British aid – an emerging great power that has its own space programme and a rapidly expanding military, at a time when Britain apparently cannot even afford key elements of its own armed forces. Indeed, London's India policy seemed to have more to do with the power of the British-Indian vote in certain marginal constituencies, which demonstrated eloquently the extent to which politics so often consumes strategy in Britain.

Therefore, Britain must re-learn the art of making strategy in uncertainty for it is only when the powerful make strategy that uncertainty becomes certainty. In other words, to re-visit Acheson Britain might indeed have arrived at a strategic destination of sorts in the old world, but seems utterly lost in the new world. This is partly

---

[40] In one of his first pronouncements in August 2013 the newly-appointed Chief of Defence Staff General Sir Nick Houghton warned that Britain would need in future to be more modest in its military ambitions. Report by BBC Defence Correspondent Caroline Wyatt, BBC Radio 4 "Today Programme", 22 August, 2013.

because British 'war' aims in World War Two and the Cold War were ultimately achieved. It is also partly because Britain faces no clearly defined and immediate challenge in its neighbourhood; Europe today is replete with parliamentary democracies that will never again threaten Britain and whilst Russia and Islamism are dangers they pose no immediate existential threat to the British state. However, beyond the fact of achieving past 'war aims' Britain has proved itself inept over successive administrations in shaping the actions of those democracies in support of Britain's peacetime national interests.

The ends, ways and means of British strategy in an age of profound strategic transition require the effective embrace of new power through functioning international institutions built on a Britain willing and able to generate the power and influence that shape such institutions in the British national interest. Both NSS 2015 and SDSR 2015 must reflect such a new concept of British power. That means a credible British ability to generate and engage all forms of national power; co-operative and at times coercive. Critically, renewed British strategy will also need a planning focus that can make best use of British resources given the strategic environment and the threats, challenges and risks that Britain is likely to face.

The danger in a world in which the means of destruction have become so broad is that leaders are unable to provide the national strategic leadership upon which sound national strategic planning must be based. Be it climate change, the proliferation of weapons of mass destruction, drug and human trafficking, transnational crime, mass migration, inter-state competition over energy, the threat of pandemics or even the renewed geopolitical threat of inter-state war, it is hard for any liberal state these days to assess where best to focus limited resources and human capital to best effect.

That said, only recognising as much threat as one can afford is no solution either, as much of Europe is fast discovering. Rather, broad security planning is required that considers all state security assets as part of a continuum of offensive and defensive influence, built on an ability to constantly and objectively re-evaluate the level of resources that should be devoted to security and defence. National security policy must, therefore, elaborate the security end-states Britain seeks; establish a national strategy that implements policy effectively and consistently. NSS 2015 and SDSR 2015 must be central to the strategic renewal implied by such an effort.

Britain's armed forces will undoubtedly take a leading role in this process because of their experience in comprehensive security planning and SDSR 2015 must highlight such a role. However, in an age when security requires a full spectrum of capabilities – military and civilian – it is also vital that government as a whole acts as an effective mechanism for the co-ordination and synthesis of all national efforts.

A vital ally in Britain's strategic renovation will be the undoubted creative power of British society. All of the above can and will only be established in a society that understands and accepts both the challenge and the costs of security and is sufficiently resilient to cope with the attacks and set-backs that twenty-first century Britain will undoubtedly suffer. National strategy will thus require new partnerships between outside groups and actors hitherto avoided by government as being too complex or difficult to deal with. Moreover, stove-piped thinking which has too often reinforced stove-piped cultures that disaggregate British strategic effect must be rejected once and for all. Indeed, such strategic, political, bureaucratic and even cultural narrow-mindedness must end as a matter of urgency if Britain is to be secured in the twenty-first century.

For Britain, the re-balancing of powers should not presage decline and fall, but rather radical change in the generation and practice of strategy. Therefore, the first task of national strategy must be to better understand the scope and extent of strategic change that is taking place and the nature of the strategic challenges that will confront Britain over the medium-term. Thereafter, Britain must engage Europeans, Americans and partners the world-over to craft what will necessarily become a new British strategic concept for a new Britain in a new age. NSS 2015 and SDSR 2015 must provide essential platforms for such ambition.

Decline and fall is not Britain's inevitable fate, but only the conscious crafting of strategy built on a proper appreciation of the world beyond and appropriate investment in the tools of influence will afford security to the British people. Failure to invest will make the cost of insecurity far greater over time. NSS 2015 and SDSR 2015 will demonstrate to the world which direction of travel Britain has chosen, whatever the political spin that will doubtless accompany its launch. After all, it is a question of ambition.

3.

Britain's Strategic Environment

"No longer is our existence as states under threat. Now our actions are guided by a more subtle blend of mutual self-interest and moral purpose in defending the values we cherish. In the end values and interests merge".

Former Prime Minister Tony Blair[41]

The Global Race and the Value-Interest

Britain's dangerous world is one that will demand of Britain vision, leadership, creativity, commitment and agile strategy. British strategy sits at a nexus between values and interests - the value-interest – and must make a reasoned case for balance between the two precisely to avoid their confusion. The reason why Britain needs strategy should be self-evident. Prime Minister David Cameron calls it "the global race" in a world marked by growing hyper-competition between states and hyper-hatreds within states and across entire regions, most notably the Middle East, Africa and Asia. [42] Such competition is implicitly reflected in Russia's use of hybrid warfare in Ukraine, and the emergence of the ISIS super-insurgency across the Middle East focused.

The problem for Britain is that the European region in which it sits is marked by low growth and declining relative wealth and power. According to a 2010 Citigroup report, Asia alone accounts today for some 24% of world trade, 42% by 2030 and 46% by 2050.[43]

---

[41] Speech to the Economic Club, Chicago, 22 April 1999, see www.pbs.org/newshour/bb/international-jan-june99-blair_doctrine 4-23/
[42] Prime Minister David Cameron first used the term "The Global Race" in a speech to the Confederation for British Industry on 19 November 2012 entitled "Get Britain on the rise, to compete in the global race". https://www.gov.uk/government/news/prime-ministers-cbi-speech
[43] See "US to fall behind India in world trade, report says", USA Today, 7 March 2011 http://usatoday30.usatoday.com/money/world/2011-07-03-cnbc-us-trade-india_n.htm

Whereas, whilst Western Europe represented 48% of world trade in 1990, 34% in 2013 it could fall to 19% in 2030 and 15% by 2050.[44] The relatively weaker a state becomes the more important strategy and the greater the need to exploit all of its resources. This is particularly important as illiberal power rises to challenge liberal power, which could well become the signature friction of the twenty-first century.

A journey (strategic survey) through Britain's rapidly-changing strategic environment is necessarily long and complicated and reinforces the need for effective British strategy. Such strategy will need to be agile and clever if it is to magnify and focus Britain's influence in an exceedingly complex world in which London will need to bring real power to bear if the institutions that will be the main vehicle for British influence are to be effective. Therefore, in the midst of such strategic flux generating clear national strategy must be Britain's defining challenge in the early part of the twenty-first century and both NSS 2015 and SDSR 2015 must rise to meet that challenge. Indeed, strategy and the knowledge and understanding upon which it is established, will be vital to understanding where and how best to apply British influence.

However, the crafting of strategy that can help government apply to effect all the necessary tools and instruments available to the British state will not be easy. Britain's post World War Two retreat into a strategic no man's land – neither in Europe nor the world beyond - allied to the abandonment of traditional strategic analysis has left London unable to fashion evidence-based national strategy. Too often the consistent confusion of values with interests has prevented Britain from generating a big picture understanding of the world as it is, rather than as London would like it to be. This has prevented Britain from establishing its contemporary strategic place and role and quantifying its interests, which has in turn accelerated and accentuated Britain's decline.

London must now make some very hard choices but how, why and where? Of course, many of the 'choices' available to London still

---

[44] Ibidem.

depend on the future strategic orientation of the United States which is probably as unclear about its role as at any time since 1945. Tony Blair's one-time Chief of Staff Jonathon Powell writes, "If, after Iraq and Afghanistan, the US were to enter another lengthy period of isolationism, Britain and other countries like us would be the principal losers. No other power in the world can intervene with the force and technological advantages of the US. The rising powers like China and India will fill some of the vacuum left by the US in their regions, but Europe will be expected to deal with its own neighbourhood, including Eastern Europe and the former Soviet Union and North Africa."[45] That is surely correct, but far from waiting for America to make up its strategic mind Britain needs to be able to influence Washington's choices. Such influence will rest to a significant extent upon the strength of Britain's armed forces. SDSR 2015 will thus be a strategic narrative for others as much as a planning document for Britain's Future Force.

SDSR 2015 will also need to demonstrate that Britain understands the choices it must make. There are four strengths a state needs if it is to deal successfully with the strategically unforeseeable – versatility, flexibility/agility, capability and credibility. Credibility is of particular importance - with friends, partners, but above all adversaries. The British must be far clearer about the world in which they reside and the opportunities, risks and dangers it both generates and poses. This is not least because the immaturity of emerging state power is generating a global balance of power more liable to flux than any of the four very different European strategic eras between 1870 and 1989, all of which collapsed.[46] Critically, SDSR 2015 must confront the dynamic change that is radically re-organising global power and the alliances and regimes necessary to manage it.

---

[45] Powell, Jonathon (2010) "The New Machiavelli: How to Wield Power in the Modern World" (London: The Bodley Head) p. 277

[46] For perhaps still the most effective discussion of the balance of power see Kennedy, Paul (1988) "The Rise and Fall of the Great Powers: Economic Change and Military Conflict From 1500-2000". (New York: Random House)

There are seven major strategic issues Britain must confront in today's world: energy security; geopolitics and new emerging power-houses such as China and India; recalcitrant and/or revisionist powers such as Iran and Russia; the retreat of the Western-inspired state across much of the Middle East in the face of Islamism and immature liberalism; humanitarian crises with implications for regional-strategic balance, particularly in Europe's neighbourhood; the withdrawal from Afghanistan and its implications; and the proliferation and use of weapons of mass destruction (WMD).

Another set of challenges will emerge from wider globalisation and humanitarian crises, such as cyber-crime and threats to critical national infrastructure, challenges to national social cohesion, drug and human trafficking, pandemics and the proliferation of small arms.

Energy Security

How will Britain ensure and protect the secure supply of energy? British Socialist Aneurin Bevan once remarked, "This Island is almost made of coal and surrounded by fish. Only an organising genius could produce a shortage of coal AND fish at the same time".[47] Today, Bevan would probably have added shale oil and gas to his irony given the significant amounts of both upon which Britain (particularly England) is apparently sitting. Global hyper-competition reinforces the pressing need for energy security. Shale oil and gas could profoundly change the geopolitical balance between suppliers and *demandeurs* of energy, as both Russia and Saudi Arabia are discovering to their cost. Indeed, Russia's actions in Ukraine and the EU's at best anaemic response to Moscow's aggression have demonstrated the danger of over-reliance on one source of energy.

Like most of Europe Britain is increasingly reliant on a few unstable and/or unreliable suppliers. This vulnerability has been acutely aggravated by the failure of successive governments to take a strategic view on nuclear power and other forms of energy, such as

---

[47] See www.famousquotes.com/author/aneurin-bevan

renewables.[48] The risk is that energy could act as a danger multiplier in the coming years. Energy insecurity will also inevitably lead to competition with much of the developing *demandeur* economies (China and India) and likely further fuel popular pressure for change in the supplier economies in the Middle East. Perhaps the most important strategic change for Britain could be an America that becomes energy self-sufficient, as this would alter many of the bedrock assumptions about the role and reliability of the Americans as the last resort guarantor of British and European security upon which British national strategy is built.

The threat to Britain's energy security is apparent from the figures. Exxon Mobil in their 2012 report "2020 The Outlook for Energy: A View to 2040" estimated that global energy demand could be 30% higher in 2040 than 2010 with a world population will 9 billion larger. Demand in OECD states will be flat, but demand in non-OECD countries could grow by about 60%. Fossil fuels will still meet 80% of the total energy needs whilst the demand for natural gas will increase by 60% by 2040.[49]

What options does Britain have? A 2013 British Geological Survey report suggests that Britain's shale oil and gas reserves could be enough to make the British energy self-sufficient for many years to come, with up to 1,300 trillion cubic feet of gas alone.[50] However, a fractious debate is now breaking out within and without government between those who see shale oil and gas as a strategic asset, and those who suggest Britain should act as an example to the world by rejecting the use of fossil fuels on environmental grounds. It is

---

[48] Under the title of "Maintaining UK Energy Security", on 27 June, 2013 the British Government published an official study that suggests under the eleven counties of Northern England there are up to 40 trillion cubic metres of shale gas (1300 trillion cubic feet). See https://www.gov.uk/government/news/estimates-of-shale-gas-reserves-in-north-of-england-published-alongside-a-package-of-community-benefits.
[49] See Exxon Mobil (2012) "2020 The Outlook for Energy: A View to 2040". (London:ExxonMobil)p1
http://www.exxonmobil.co.uk/Corporate/files/news_pub_eo2012.
[50] See "UK shale gas reserves 'greater than thought'" BBC News, 27 June, 2013, http://www.bbc.co.uk/news/business-23069499

perhaps the most egregious example of the confusion of values with a very clear national interest. Hopefully, common sense will break out and a new balance will be struck between energy security and the development and use of alternative fuel sources.

However, the very real danger exists that a typically-British protracted internal debate will ensue over what represents 'green' energy. The paralysis in government caused by such a debate will not only prevent a coherent, strategic approach to filling Britain's looming energy gap but likely reveal again the profound tension between strategy and politics at the top of British government.

Writing in the *Daily Telegraph* on the 11th August, 2013 Prime Minister Cameron wrote, "If we don't back this technology, we will miss a massive opportunity to help families with their bills and make our country more competitive. Without it, we could lose ground in the tough global race".[51] Cameron is right. However, pubic anxiety cannot be ignored. In 2012 concerns were expressed in Lancashire that the use of high-pressure water (fracking) to drive oil and gas reserves up and out of the ground had caused small earthquakes (a Beatles song?). This fracas has since been followed by 2013 protests against test drilling in Balcombe, West Sussex.

What about the geopolitics of shale? If Americans and Europeans are major producers and consumers then one of the main causes of systemic friction would have been removed. There is growing hyper-competition over resources between the consuming democracies and the ever-more-consuming oligarchies, such as China. What makes this competition potentially dangerous is that power in China and other oligarchies is legitimised by economic growth rather than the vote. Such friction could well become another signature threat of this century. Equally, a shift in the balance of energy power away from the producers, be it Russia or the Middle East, may also make it easier to find political solutions to many contentions, not least between Israel and the Palestinians (although it is a big 'if'). As for Russia, Moscow would become one

---

[51] http://www.telegraph.co.uk/news/politics/1023666/We-cannot-afford-to-miss-out-on-shale-gas.html

producer amongst many and would therefore have to compete for exports on price...and behaviour, something which is undoubtedly concentrating the minds of the narrow Kremlin clique who advise President Putin.

Building BRICS?

What consideration must Britain give to the new geopolitics? Brazil, Russia, India, China and South Africa - the BRICS - represent 25.9% of the world's landmass, 43% of the population and 17% of global trade.[52] The UN Development Programme suggests that by 2020 the combined economic output of three leading developing countries alone – Brazil, China and India – will surpass the aggregate production of Canada, France, Germany, Italy and the United States, although there are many potential shocks that could prevent the painless realisation of such an analysis. At the April 2014 sixth annual summit of the BRICS in Brazil, a new BRICS Bank was created, under the catchy 1960s throwback title of "Partnership for Development, Integration and Industrialisation". The aim of the BRICS Bank is clear; to counterbalance the western-dominated International Monetary Fund and to plug a gap in development-financing caused by the West's financial and economic woes.

The geopolitical consequences of such an initiative are potentially the most interesting aspect of the BRICS grouping. On the strategic face of it the Brazil summit seemed a natural extension of Chinese President Xi Jingping's Kissingeresque March 2013 visit to Moscow. China and Russia clearly think in terms of classical Kennanesque Cold War Realism and thus see the strategic game with the West as ultimately a zero sum game – there can be only one winner. This sense of an emergent, new geopolitical divide was reinforced by the March 2014 gas deal between China and Russia, albeit very much on Chinese terms. Clearly, Moscow is in urgent need of new allies given the sharp deterioration in Russia's relationship with the West since the annexation of Crimea in March 2014 and its ongoing aggression in eastern Ukraine.

---

[52] See BBC News, 25 March, 2013, "Brics nations meet to cement relationships" www.bbc.co.uk/business-21923874

However, for all the clear ambitions of China, and to a markedly lesser extent Russia, the five BRICS countries are still divided on many issues and Britain and the West can and must exploit such divisions. Brazil and India come from that rather woolly tradition of non-alignment and neither would wish to see themselves as part of a Chinese sphere of influence.[53] Today, India is emerging in its own right and is as much a regional-strategic competitor of China as a partner. Brazil fits pretty much into the same category as India and views itself as the emerging leader of Latin America. As for South Africa, the weakest of the BRICS, the ANC-led government is instinctively drawn to any form of non-alignment that has a vague anti-Western tinge which is reinforced by Pretoria's desperate need of Chinese capital.

If the BRICS become seen as too overtly a part of a new *Chinasphere* it will rapidly fall apart. At the 2013 Durban BRICS summit each member put some $10bn (€7.8bn) into the BRICS Bank, which was indicative in and of itself. Whilst this figure represented some 0.1% of China's GDP, it was some 2% of South African GDP.[54] Therefore, the cost-benefits would appear on the face of it to be sharply different, especially as Pretoria sees itself as a big net consumer of aid. For the moment the BRICS will remain a loose arrangement rather than a counter-balancing mechanism to the West, even if over the longer-term the BRICS countries will clearly enjoy greater influence. However, it is very much open to question if they will do so collectively.

---

[53] George Kennan wrote in 1947 "Russia will remain economically a vulnerable, and in a certain sense an impotent nation, capable of exporting its enthusiasm and of radiating the strange charm of its primitive political vitality but unable to back up those articles of export by the real evidence of material power and prosperity". See "X" (George Kennan) "The Sources of Soviet Conduct", Foreign Affairs, originally published in June 1947, reprinted in Vol. 65, No 4. (Spring 1987), p. 856.
[54] See BBC News, 25 March, 2013, "Brics nations meet to cement relationships" www.bbc.co.uk/business-21923874

China

How will Britain prepare for an illiberal, strategic China with armed forces to match? THE major strategic change to the international system, with which the West and Britain must contend, is the emergence of a capitalist/nationalist illiberal China as a global economic superpower armed with the potential to become a global military superpower. China's strategic aim is ultimately a China-centric Asia, even if for the moment China remains a massive developing power that only in time could become a superpower. However, to realise such a goal China must also overcome many inherent weaknesses. During David Cameron's December 2013 trade visit to China the Chinese Premier Li Keqiang described China's relationship with Britain as an "indispensable partnership". Of course, the phrase was meant more in flattery than as a reflection of how the Chinese leadership really sees Britain – which is not at all flattering.

Ironically, Cameron's visit to China suggests he has finally fallen on a "Cameron Doctrine" of sorts – mercantilism. Mercantilism is where a state establishes strategy on the idea that a positive balance of trade is a strategic end in and of itself, and that the role of the state is to support such efforts. If correct Cameron's mercantilism is ironic to say the least in that it was mercantilism that drove Britain's imperial expansion and led to the Opium Wars of the 1840s with then-imperial China, which-once-and-for all ended China as an imperial power. Long of memory the Opium Wars are something the Chinese have neither forgotten nor forgiven.

Critically, Beijing believes its time as a world power has come and the figures certainly support that assertion. According to American investment bankers Goldman Sachs, China's gross domestic product (GDP) surpassed that of Britain in 2005 and Germany in 2008, and could even surpass the Americans as early as 2016. According to "The World Order in 2050", an April 2010 report by the Carnegie Foundation for International Peace, by 2050 the three so-called 'mega-economies' China, India and the US will enjoy a combined GDP worth 70% more than the combined economies of all the remaining G20 states.[55]

China clearly has the ambition to become an alternative global power pole to the US in a new bipolar order. The November 2013 Chinese unilateral declaration of an air defence zone over the disputed Diaoyu/Senkaku islands is clearly part of an attempt to exert regional-strategic pressure on Japan, and the 2014 construction of a base on the Fiery Cross Reef suggests wider strategic ambitions.

At the start of his visit to Moscow Chinese President Xi Jingping said that the "two countries were most important strategic allies who spoke a common language".[56] Xi's visit to Moscow took place just over forty years on from Henry Kissinger's famous 1971 visit to Beijing that forced the then Soviet Union onto the strategic defensive. China's new strategy is almost a mirror-image of the Nixon-Kissinger *démarche* and will inevitably lead to further friction with the US. Indeed, China's expansionism is already leading to adjustments in American and indeed Russian strategy, both of which have profound strategic implications for Britain and the wider Europe.

Kissinger's 1971 visit to China was set against the backdrop of a Nixon administration desperate to extract itself from a failing Vietnam War. Kissinger, the grand architect of Cold War *Realpolitik*, wanted to force the Soviet Union to look both east and west – a form of strategic *'zweifrontenskrieg'* (two-front war). Moscow was at the time embroiled in a full-scale border war with China, a supposed Communist partner. By forcing the Soviet Union to face the prospect of a *'zweifrontenskrieg'*, Kissinger was applying lessons from the history of his native Germany to US grand strategy.

Critically, Xi seems also to have understood Kissinger's dictum that "no country can act wisely in every part of the globe at every moment of time".[57] The aim of Chinese grand strategy is certainly

[55] See Dadush, U. & Stancil B (2010) "The World Order in 2050", (New York: Carnegie Endowment for International Peace) p 9.
[56] See BBC News Asia, "China's President XI Jingping heads to Russia". 22 March, 2013 http://bbc.co.uk/news/world-asia-21892614
[57] For a fascinating contemporary discussion of Kissinger's foreign policy views in which this quote appears see Brandon, Donald (1969) "Henry Kissinger's

not to trigger a war with the Americans, but to demonstrate to Washington that China is a world power and must be respected as such. Equally, there can be no doubt Beijing is also seeking to complicate American strategic calculation the world over by forcing over-stretch upon the United States. Indeed, ancient Chinese strategist Sun Tzu would have recognised and approved of contemporary Beijing's strategic logic; force an opponent to confront so many options over such time and distance that to all intents and purposes they render themselves weak through a surfeit of uncertainty.

The timing of Xi's 2014 visit to Moscow was impeccable. There are of course perfectly legitimate reasons for reasonably close Chinese-Russian relations and differences that separate Beijing and Moscow must not be under-estimated. They are partners in the Shanghai Co-operation Organisation (SCO), China is the world's biggest energy consumer whilst Russia is the biggest energy provider, trade between the two countries is booming and is now worth some $88bn or €60bn per annum.[58] However, Xi's visit was also grand strategy in the making and must be seen as such. China's aim is to lead those powers that seek to counter-balance the American-led West, and to that end Beijing intends to forge relationships that exploit American uncertainty and Europe's precipitous decline.

Kissinger famously suggested that, "If you don't know where you are going, every road will get you nowhere".[59] Clearly, Britain must not fall into the trap of concluding that legitimate Chinese ambitions are a precursor to conflict and London seems determined not to do so. However, neither Americans nor Europeans should ignore Chinese intent or its burgeoning power, wealth or military capability.

Approach to Foreign Policy" in the Carnegie Council on Foreign Relations "World View"ofMarch1969.
http://worldview.carnegiecouncil.org/archive/worldview/1969/03/4803.html/_res/id=sa_File/
[58] BBC News Asia, "China's President XI Jingping heads to Russia". 22 March, 2013 http://bbc.co.uk/news/world-asia-21892614
[59] http://www.brainyquote.com/quotes/authors/henry_a_kissinger.html

In policy terms China will no doubt wish to co-operate with the US in areas such as technology and finance if it is to China's advantage. On the other hand, China will likely seek to constrain US strategic options and compete with Washington for regional-strategic supremacy. Certainly, the extent of Chinese electronic, cyber and other intelligence activities, does not suggest a China that sees itself as either a friend or a committed strategic partner of the West. At best China will be a vaguely-constructive competitor at least as long as such co-operation is in the Chinese interest.

Therefore, President Xi's stated ambitions, the November 2013 social and economic reforms agreed at the Communist Party "Plenum", Chinese spying activities and the territorial disputes with Japan, all suggest a China that believes that some form of future strategic competition with both the US and the wider West is sooner or later inevitable. This impetus should not be over-stated, but nor can it be ignored.

Given Chinese ambitions there has been much wishful thinking in Europe about future relations with China and Russia, which was revealed by Moscow's 2014 seizure of Ukraine-Crimea. Neither China nor Russia is a liberal-democracy, and neither has a tradition of peaceful co-existence. Moreover, nationalism has replaced Communism as the essential political creed in both countries with both Beijing and Moscow likely to use whatever comparative advantages they believe they have in the pursuit of very narrowly-defined national interests. Again, such an approach will focus first on establishing regional rather than global dominance, but friction with the West is inevitable.

The specific geopolitical implications of China's rise are yet to become clear. Indeed, until the struggle between the Communist Party leadership in Beijing and the capitalists in Shanghai and Hong Kong is finally won (by the latter), it is hard to discern the moment when China will move from economic powerhouse to military superpower. However, that is the likely goal, particularly so as the People's Liberation Army (PLA) becomes ever more influential in Chinese power politics – both internally and externally. [60] President

Xi has made it clear his intention that China must become a first-rate military power and that Beijing assert its interests with force if needs be. Therefore, British interests will be profoundly affected by the rise of China, not least because the US will be forced to re-focus its main security effort on Asia-Pacific rather than Europe. It is a shift which will re-impose on Britain the need to think globally, systemically and strategically.

It is the combination of ambition, instability, nationalism and the determination of the Party to control power that makes China hard to read. Equally, China is no monolith. Richard N. Haass, former Policy Director at the US State Department, highlights the domestic drivers of Chinese instability. "Domestic pressures – the need to raise hundreds of millions more Chinese out of poverty, growing resentment over income and wealth inequality, the need to keep growth rates high – are also pushing China to find something to complement, if not replace, export-led growth. The result is that China is in the early days of transition, one in which economic growth will increasingly have to stem from demand at home. Like all transitions, economic transition is easier to call than to bring about".[61]

China and Its Neighbours

What role if any does Britain have in supporting allies in Asia-Pacific? Beijing worries publicly about other powers seeking to 'contain' China, in much the same way that the US successfully contained Soviet Russia during the Cold War. Paradoxically, China's fear could be self-fulfilling if Beijing continues to use a heavy hand to impose its will in East Asia, particularly in the East and South China Seas.

---

[60] The power of Chinese nationalism was witnessed by this author during a brief stint living in Hong Kong in the early 1980s.
[61] Haass, Richard N. (2011) "China's Greatest Threat is Internal", In the Financial Times, December 28, 2011. http://www.cfr.org/china/chinas-greatest-threat-internal/p26930

In a sense China's position in Asia is somewhat similar to that of Germany in Europe, without the stabilising and ameliorating institutional framework of the EU. Much like the European pecking order did much to shape the nineteenth century world, the twenty-first century world order will reflect much the shape of power in East Asia. Nothing is more likely to engender an anti-Chinese regional coalition than a heavy-handed China that makes a mockery of its so-called foreign policy paradigm "strategic harmony". Any such coalition would inevitably and invariably draw in the Americans and in time could reverse the very globalisation that has made China powerful, as multinational corporations withdraw from China and 're-shore' in the West.

Clearly, the East China Sea is fast becoming the hub of a strategic contest that could well define the twenty-first century; the struggle for power dominance in East Asia. The immediate prize is (as so often) oil and gas. China estimates that between one hundred and one hundred and sixty billion barrels of oil lie beneath the East China Sea, with a possible further twenty-eight billion barrels lying beneath the South China Sea.[62]

Equally, important though oil and gas may be to resource-starved Asian economies, the many disputes in which China is embroiled with its neighbours are not just about exclusive control of hydrocarbons, but also concern geopolitics and the future regional-strategic pecking order in East Asia. The conflict with Japan is a case in point. Recent Chinese-Japanese tensions over the Diaoyu/Senkaku islands are partly driven by the island's location in the Xihu/Okinawa trough basin with an estimated twenty billion barrels of extractable oil believed to rest beneath the islands. However, the Chinese have claimed the islands since at least the fourteenth century, whilst Japan asserted control over them in 1895 as a stepping stone on the road to Tokyo's then imperial ambitions. This eventually led to Japan's brutal 1937 invasion and occupation of Manchuria (China), the 1940 Greater East Asia Co-Prosperity Sphere and eventually the 1941 Pacific War. The Americans took control in 1945 with the defeat of imperial Japan, but handed them

---

[62] Author's own research

back to Tokyo in 1971 to ease Japanese concerns about the Nixon-Kissinger rapprochement with Mao's China.

Today, it is China that is exerting its regional-strategic economic and military muscle. China has established the self-declared Exclusive Economic Zone or EEZ, and although the Zone is ill-defined it nominally extends to more than two hundred miles off the Chinese coast, with some Chinese maps showing the EEZ extending right across both the South and East China Seas, from Vietnam to Japan.

China also disputes the sovereignty of the Spratly Islands with the Philippines, in particular the Reed Bank on which a British company is currently surveying for oil and which is regularly harassed by Chinese vessels. China is also exerting pressure on *Petro Vietnam* as it searches for oil and gas in Hanoi's own self-declared EEZ off the Vietnamese coast. In October 2011, China and Vietnam signed an agreement that established principles for resolving maritime issues, but only time will demonstrate its utility and indeed its endurance.

However, it is Taiwan (Republic of China) that is the most likely flashpoint of future conflict between China and the US. Sooner or later the impulse to 'solve' the Taiwan question militarily could well prove irresistible for Beijing. Indeed, to some extent Beijing views Taiwan much like Moscow views Crimea – a region that is an integral part of the country given away to another in a fit of weakness. That was then and this is now and any conflict over Taiwan would lead to a rapid acceleration of an already intense arms race in East Asia.

It is the mix of rapid growth, ancient regional grievances, nationalism, modernising militaries, advanced technologies and a lack of indigenous fossil fuels that renders East Asia the world's most dangerous region. There is also the very real possibility of strategic spill-over in the event of a major war from which Britain could neither insulate nor isolate itself. Therefore, London will at least need to consider how best to protect Britain's long-term strategic interests in the region, both directly and in support of the US, Japan, Australia, India, South Korea and other regional allies and partners. Naturally, Britain will and must rely on others with a more direct stake in Asia-Pacific to take the lead, as British interests must be clearly distinguished from any residual imperial reflex. However, Britain could be badly damaged by a war in Asia in which not one British soldier fought. And, for all Britain's contemporary decline many in Asia would still expect Britain to play a role, not least as a P5 member of the UN Security Council.

Russia

What must Britain do to counter an aggressive Russia? On 1 July, 2014 President Putin laid out Russia's foreign and security policy priorities to Russian ambassadors and Heads of Mission at a closed door meeting in Moscow. Three themes stood out: the primacy of the Russian national interest, a specifically Russian interpretation of international law and a new European security order. President Putin has repeatedly expressed his Russian-centric world-view in open fora over many years, and yet neither American nor European leaders have appeared to have believed him. Indeed, as early as the 2007 Munich Security Conference, Putin accused the United States of seeking world domination to justify a beefing-up of the Russian state.

In a 2008 speech in St Peterburg Putin also laid out three principles of Russia-centric European security which presaged the 2014 Ukraine crisis: there can be no security at the expense of another (Russia); there can be no action within or by military alliances or coalitions (NATO) that would weaken overall security; and no military alliance (NATO) should expand at the expense of another (Russia). Moreover, at the 2008 NATO Bucharest Summit President Putin told a stunned US President George W. Bush that as far as Russia was concerned Ukraine was not even a country.

In other words, President Putin has been entirely consistent both in his stated world-view and in his determination to pursue aggressively the Russian national interest as he sees it. In his July, 2014 statement Putin also used strong language to reinforce the lengths Moscow would go to assure its interests and 'protect' those who regard themselves as Russian, including the use of so-called "self-defence".

In 2014 Putin blamed the US and EU for forcing Russia to intervene in Ukraine, although he was careful not to include certain European countries, most notably Germany. Specifically, Putin implied that an American-led policy of NATO deterrence was in fact a continuation of the Cold War and told assembled Russian diplomats that Moscow would never "abandon" Crimea to "nationalist militants" or allow NATO "to change" the balance of power in the Black Sea. He also continued with his now well-established theme that the United States is seeking global domination.

In 2014, President Putin also reinforced his efforts to further divide an already weak and divided Europe. He blamed Ukraine's 2014-elected President Poroshenko for the breakdown of a ceasefire in Ukraine in spite of the best diplomatic efforts of Germany and France. He also accused the US of blackmailing France with penalties against its banks and linked those threats to then French plans to deliver two advanced assault ships to the Russian Navy.

In the July statement Putin also revealed a long-standing and apparently genuinely-held frustration over what he sees as US hypocrisy. Russia, Putin asserted, sought the mandatory application of international law "without double standards", i.e. no action without a UN Security Council mandate over which of course Moscow has a veto. President Putin also emphasised the continued expansion of Russia's armed forces and the reinforcement of Moscow's efforts to strengthen its sphere of influence as part of a new balance of power. Moscow would also seek to exert influence over states in the former Soviet Union and beyond through the Commonwealth of Independent States, a Eurasian Economic Union and the Shanghai Co-operation Organisation.

Therefore, in the face of Russia's determination to assert what it sees as its vital interests via strategic competition Britain along with the rest of Europe must be clear about Moscow's strengths and weaknesses. In fact, Russia is a declining power with a complex population that must be governed over nine time zones. According to the *CIA World Factbook* Russia's economy is roughly the same size as Britain's with a population of over one-hundred and forty million people with a GDP per capita that ranks only seventy-seventh in the world.[63] For all that President Putin still aims to re-establish Russia as an alternative power pole in Europe to Germany and what it sees as a German-led EU. That indeed is the implicit and not-so-implicit message from Moscow given its annexation of significant parts of Ukraine and its unilateral re-ordering of twenty-first century European borders. The greatest danger posed to Britain by a military well-armed Moscow is not Russia's strength but its growing economic and political weakness.

Russia today is a dangerous cocktail of over-centralised power, nostalgia, weakness and elite paranoia, allied to a strong sense of historic grievance and entitlement. Critically, with some 20% of all Russian public expenditure now being devoted to military modernisation Russia's innovative use of force is the most pressing concern for Britain, particularly its developing use of hybrid/non-linear warfare and disinformation campaigns designed to keep Europe and the wider West split and politically off-balance. Moreover, Russia is led by a traditionalist clique organised around a strong man president who is difficult to predict, more so since the 2015 oil price crash. Although facing a powerful combination of political, economic and social problems Russia remains a serious systemic strategic player that cannot be ignored. Worse, the re-emergence of Russian prickliness has gone hand in hand with the growing dependence of much of the rest of Europe on Russian energy.

Initially, the EU fell apart over what to do about Russia's Ukrainian adventure. The motley collection of asset freezes and travel bans the EU imposed on those close to President Putin fooled no-one, and certainly no-one in Moscow. Equally predictably Britain and France fell out over the nature and the extent of sanctions to be imposed on Moscow. In July 2014 France accused Britain of hypocrisy over London's demand that Paris halt the €1.2bn sale of the two state-of-the-art French assault ships to Russia. French Foreign Minister Laurent Fabius not unreasonably pointed out that Britain had been

---

[63] CIA World Factbook 2013 figures. https://www.cia.gov/library/publications/the-world-factbook/geos/rs.html

78

far too unquestioning about the provenance of Russian money flowing into London. It was also an embarrassment to the British that just as Prime Minister Cameron was making his July 2014 call for an extension to his March 2014 ban on arms sales it was revealed that London still had some 252 active arms export licenses worth some £132m ($222m/€166m) for the sale of weapons to Russia.

However, European partners have slowly reinforced the sanctions and most importantly Germany seems to have lost patience with a dissembling Kremlin. Finally, in November 2014 France suspended the transfer of the ships to Russia. Weighing in at 21,500 tons the *Mistral*-class ships are state-of-the-art marine amphibious command and assault ships that for the first time would have given Russia the ability to launch from the sea 450 special and specialised troops supported by helicopters and tanks. Although Russia promised not to use them in its 'Near Abroad' the two ships could have been deployed anywhere around Europe, from the High North to the Baltic Sea, from the Black Sea to the Mediterranean.

As Russia flexes its strategic muscles Britain has become the target of choice on several occasions for the Kremlin and Russian nationalists, most spectacularly (and allegedly) with the November 2006 London murder of Russian émigré Alexander Litvinenko, allegedly by an individual close to the Kremlin. The focus on Britain by the Kremlin is paradoxically flattering and concerning. Like their Iranian counterparts, many of the so-called *Siloviki* (state security apparatchiks) see Britain as a metaphor for the US.[64] Indeed, by targeting Britain Moscow can send a message to Washington that is not directly injurious to American interests.

Equally, Russia is clearly intent on challenging American interests. One of Russia's long-held strategic aims has been the need to maintain a warm water naval base that could enable Russian

---

[64] It was a flattering illusion but for much of the Cold War both Moscow and Tehran subscribed far more of the West's cleverness to London than was in any way deserved. It is certainly true that the struggle between British Intelligence and the KGB was hard fought but much of the prejudice on the Russian side can be traced back to the Great Game of the nineteenth century as Russia fought and failed to de-stabilise British India.

influence in the Mediterranean and the Middle East. Sevastopol has long provided just such a facility for the Black Seas Fleet, which is to all intents and purposes, a Russian Mediterranean Fleet. The nature of the Russian military operation in Crimea and the use of Special Forces to establish a bridgehead at Simferopol and Sevastopol Airports are also indicative of the direction of travel of Russia's concept of force. Indeed, the 28 December, 2014 update to Russia's military doctrine highlighted *Masirovska*, the use of ambiguous warfare or secret war to achieve Russia's political ends. *Masirovska* points to Russian use of expeditionary operations to create and exploit local unrest in areas where significant Russian-speaking populations reside.

Russian assertiveness is unlikely to change, so long as President Putin is in power, and power continues to be centralized on the President's Office via the National Security Council. Moreover, the Kremlin will continue to have a love-hate relationship with Western powers, dependent on the rest of Europe economically, but occasionally resorting to traditional anti-Western reflexes to mask the inherent instability and weakness of the Russian state from the Russian people. Certainly, the modernisation of Russia's armed forces is helping to promote a seductive idea amongst many Russians that Moscow can re-establish a sphere of influence over Russia's 'near abroad', particularly in central Asia, the southern Caucasus and possibly even Eastern Europe.

For all his delusions of national Russian grandeur President Putin understands power, weakness and opportunity, which explains his two-fold strategy: to decouple the US (and to a lesser extent the UK) from the security of Continental Europe; and to create a new Russian-centric European sphere of influence. Given Germany's strategic ambivalence towards the US as evidenced by a 2014 spying scandal in which Berlin accused Washington of spying and the damage done by Edward Snowden President Putin still believes he has just such an opportunity.

Equally, for all President Putin's ambitions Russia does not at present pose a real existential threat to Britain. And, Moscow has legitimate strategic and regional concerns of which Britain must also be cognisant. Indeed, as one of three European outlier powers Britain may on occasions share a convergence of interest with both Russia and Turkey, if the EU continues to integrate away from Britain. Therefore, and only if and when a just settlement to the Ukraine crisis is reached, Britain must seek to work constructively with Russia on, for example, a successor treaty for the Conventional Forces Europe (CFE) treaty, whilst at one and the same time confronting Russia over its aggressive behaviour. Britain must also continue to provide strategic reassurance to Eastern European allies, and confirm that Britain will indeed fulfil all of its NATO collective defence obligations.[65]

Furthermore, Britain must never accept that Russia has 'special rights' in Europe or that Moscow should be permitted to re-establish an extended sphere of influence over Britain's allies and/or partners. Sovereign choice by all states in the Euro-Atlantic security space is a fundamental principle underpinning both NATO and the EU which Britain must firmly uphold.

Therefore, whilst Britain must be sensitive to Russian concerns over future enlargements of both NATO and the EU, border disputes in its region, missile defence and the modernisation of NATO's strategic defence architecture, Moscow can enjoy no veto. Rather, Britain must emphasise that none of the West's efforts to enhance security in Europe are aimed at Russia *per se*. And, that Russia could still become a vital security partner in the fight against dangerous instability in all its forms if a new political accommodation can be established between Russia and the West. Certainly (and subject to Russian behaviour), Britain should seek with its North American and European allies to transform the relationship over time with Russia

---

[65] The CFE Treaty entered into force in 1992 but was modified in 1997 to account for the move away from blocs of states so that conventional forces could be measured nationally. It was a classical Cold War arms control treaty aimed at actual reduction and destruction of conventional munitions, on-site inspection, periodic exchange of detailed information and the opportunity for challenge inspections. See, Auton, Graeme P. "Multilateral Security Regimes: The Politics of CFE and CSBMs" in McKenzie Mary, M. & Loedel, Peter H. (1998) "The Promise and Reality of European Security Co-operation: States, Interests and Institutions". (Westport: Praeger)

into one of constructive engagement, built on mutual respect for international law, respect for sovereignty, the joint fight against terrorism and the mutual pursuit of financial and security stability.

Britain and its allies must also confront the many inner-contradictions in their collective approach to Russia. Americans and Europeans (and indeed Europeans and Europeans) still suffer from many conflicting approaches to dealing with Russia, which the Ukraine Crisis has highlighted. At the very least, Britain must push for a strong collective stance in the face of repeated Russian attempts to undermine NATO, including the establishment of clear criteria for judging Russian policy that could help distinguish between the constructive and the destructive. For example, whilst Russian proposals to strengthen the Organisation for Security and Co-operation in Europe (OSCE) were rightly welcomed, the 2010 Russian proposal for a New Security Treaty that threatened to undermine NATO was properly resisted.[66] Indeed, any Russian attempt to marginalise NATO or to interfere in the sovereign rights of states on Russia's borders will and must be resisted firmly by Britain.

The conflict with Russia over Ukraine is essentially one of principle. Britain must never accept the idea of a Russian sphere of influence. It is also a conflict over capability and SDSR 2015 must reflect that. Britain must also avoid strategic irresponsibility by offering commitments that cannot be defended. For example, NATO could not credibly extend an Article 5 collective defence commitment to Georgia, even if NATO's Open Door policy remains a quintessential part of the commitment to a Europe whole, free and at peace. Even if Britain maintains in principle the idea that Georgia could one day become a NATO member it would be irresponsible to extend a collective defence commitment to Georgia until an assessment has

---

[66] On 29 November 2009 then Russian President Medvedev unveiled his proposed European Security Treaty. The stated aim was to ensure that no European state or institution could act in a way that could impact on others without prior agreement. The Russia aim was to prevent further NATO enlargement and the unilateral introduction of a limited Allied ballistic missile defence. See Charnysh, Votka (2010), "Russia Drafts European Security Pact", Arms Control Association, 1 February 2010. http://www.armscontrol.org/act/2010_01_02/EuropeanSecurity

been made of how the Alliance would and could carry out such a commitment. In any case, there is no internal consensus within NATO about future enlargements.

The Ukraine Crisis is a Russian test of British (and European) resolve. Therefore, Britain must speak softly and carry a biggish stick in its dealings with Russia and SDSR 2015 must reflect that. Critically, Britain must re-build its defences. In December 2014 Russian forces stepped up their harassment of Britain's nuclear deterrent, emboldened by the misguided decision taken in SDSR 2010 to scrap the then new MRA4 maritime patrol aircraft vital for the protection of a Continually at Sea Deterrent (CASD). Not only did the decision render vulnerable the deterrent at a stroke, SDSR 2010 sent a strategic message of weakness to Russia that Moscow has been only too happy to exploit. SDSR 2015 must correct that mistake. Indeed, Britain should be under no illusions; dealing with President Putin's Russia will continue to be difficult, complicated and uncertain.

ISIS and the Collapse of the Middle East

The Middle East is and must be central to British strategy due to its proximity and the dangers it is generating for Britain's own security and defence. However, what can and must Britain do to prevent the meltdown of the Middle East and the consequences thereafter? Herodotus, the father of history, once wrote that force has no place where there is a need of skill. In the Middle East there is a desperate need for 'skill'. On 7 August 2014, President Obama ordered air strikes against ISIS as genocide beckoned in northern Iraq. In many ways the order was testament to the failure of Western policy in the region and the threat posed by Islamic fundamentalists to Middle Eastern states. Like Europe on the eve of the 1618-1648 Thirty Years War everyone and everything is deeply connected in the region, and yet at the same time dangerously divided – what Thomas Hobbes called a war of all against all.

The 2014 conflict in Gaza and the advance of ISIS across much of northern Iraq demonstrates yet again the extent to which the entire Middle East is a political tinderbox the tragedy of which can all-too easily affect and afflict Britain. Indeed, the Middle East faces potentially the complete breakdown of the state order the British and French established in the midst of World War One with the May 2016 Sykes-Picot accord.

The symbiotic nature of conflict in the region is clear and could so easily mutate into a general struggle. Israeli forces enter Gaza following the murder of three Israeli teenagers and well over a thousand Palestinians die. Shia Iran extends its influence over Baghdad, as the Sunni Islamic State is proclaimed in parts of what used to Iraq and Syria. Saudi Arabia mobilises its forces as the Sunni-Shia split deepens across the Middle East, whilst states as far apart as Algeria, Libya and the Gulf totter in the face of Islamism and liberalism as elites and societies pull apart.

There are three fundamental and quintessential struggles that are combining to threaten peace across the region (and beyond); the state versus the anti-state; the battle for regional-strategic dominance by states, and the struggle over the interpretation of Islam within failing states. Although ostensibly about religion the Thirty Year wars (for they were wars rather than a war, much like the Middle East today) were complicated by shifting 'state' power - the Habsburgs versus the Holy Roman Empire and the European core versus the European periphery - England, Sweden and Russia. They were further complicated by growing populations and divided ideologies.

Critically, the war was triggered in 1618 by a relatively minor but nevertheless explosive event – a constitutional dispute between Protestants in Bohemia and their Catholic rulers and the destruction of a single Protestant church. What happened next was unimaginable carnage.

Similar dangerous connectivities are all too apparent across the Middle East today, particularly as notions of pan-Arabism compete and from which ISIS and a form of strategic fundamentalism have been fashioned as Arab nationalism has failed, most notably the collapse of Baathism in Syria and Iraq. ISIS is in fact an anti-state force, the very existence of which threatens all other states in the region as it seeks the destruction of the entire state system and its replacement with a Caliphate.

To many Arabs nationalism once seemed the future, part and parcel of a pan-Arabism which bore a resemblance to today's pan-Europeanism. Like its European counterpart pan-Arabism was a form of artificially-engineered nationalism fuelled and reinforced by the creation of the State of Israel in 1947. However, three crushing defeats by Israel in 1948, 1967 and 1973 helped to undermine the credibility of both the Arab 'state' and pan-Arabism in the minds of an Arab World which much like Europe today is a coalition of very different peoples and traditions. Defeat also helped Islamists offer an alternative to pan-Arabism - Sunni fundamentalism.

The Arab state has been further undermined by corrupt elites, a rapidly growing population and a profound imbalance of wealth across the region in which a few 'super-haves' face a sea of 'have next to nothings'. In states such as Saudi Arabia and the Gulf States, oil-rich conservative elites have become fabulously rich whilst at the same time reluctant to disseminate wealth too widely for fear of the reform it might trigger. Indeed, like all such elites they are fearful that reform would critically undermine their power. To buy off opposition Riyadh, in particular, has at times appealed to extreme conservatism to buttress power in return for exporting the very fundamentalism that threatens the Kingdom.

And then there is Iran. Shia-Persia Iran's regional-strategic ambition to establish itself as the dominant power has also further complicated an already flammable political landscape. Worse, in its struggle with both Israel and Saudi Arabia and through the use of proxies in Syria and Lebanon, a series of bilateral disputes have slowly morphed into one enormous confrontation over the future shape of the Middle East, focussed on the relatively small space in and around Iraq, Jordan, Lebanon and Syria. Good old-fashioned *Machtpolitik* informs much of Iran's policy but Tehran is also motivated by what it sees as a Sunni threat to Shia influence that Iran believes it controls.

Today, the Middle East is in as dangerous a state as at any time since the 1973 Yom Kippur war. Indeed, it is hard to see how the acute tension in both Arab societies and between Middle Eastern states and Israel can be resolved peacefully. The outstanding question is who will be on what side and for what reason? It would be easy to suggest that a future war would be essentially between those states of Shia extraction and those of Sunni extraction. This would have Iran and Israel on the side-lines but seeking to influence proxies in a general Arab struggle. However, the Middle East is simply not that easy. Such a scenario would be complicated by ethnic divisions within many of the states involved that are rotting from the top down, which is precisely why ISIS has appeared, gained traction and appeals to Muslim youth far beyond the region, most notably in Western Europe.

The Middle East Crisis is further complicated by renewed interference from the Great Powers – America, China, Europe, and Russia - a kind of Sykes-Picot revisited. In such circumstances a regional conflict could be triggered by what is in systemic terms a relatively minor event. Any such conflict would be long and deep with hatred and calculus causing many twists and turns. A first conflict is likely to be triggered by an unofficial, unspoken and unlikely 'coalition' of states determined to defeat ISIS. Such a coalition might include Iran, Saudi Arabia, the Gulf States, Egypt, and even by extension Israel, albeit implicitly.

However, if and when ISIS is defeated, much would remain unresolved, not least between Iran and Israel. To protect its borders and break the link between Iran and Hezbollah Israel would do all it could to establish some form of influence over whatever regime eventually emerges in Syria. Any conflict that strengthens the hand of Iran on Israel's borders would be seen by Tel Aviv as a zero-sum game. For the sake of its very survival Israel would not and could not tolerate such an outcome. In a first step on the road to securing its strategic borders Israel moved decisively in 2014 to strike Hamas in Gaza, which had lost much of its support from Egypt and Syria.

Of course, the great unknown in all of this flux is the state of the Middle Eastern state. So weak are so many Middle Eastern states that ANY conflict in which they are involved could see elites cast away. Jordan is the most obvious example, but the Arab world's most populous state Egypt is not far behind, with the al-Sisi regime seen as illegitimate and propped up by the Army. The removal of the Muslim Brotherhood from power by once General, now President al-Sisi, has not resolved Egypt's myriad challenges, just delayed an inevitable reckoning.

Logically, it would actually be in the best interest of all to avoid any such general conflict and try to contain and then weaken ISIS. However, such 'logic' would take clear vision and calm judgement, both of which are in short supply in the Middle East, together with a control over events which even the United States lacks.

Equally, the Middle East remains a region of critical interest to Britain, and as the United States is forced to pivot to Asia, the Middle East, will consume much of Britain's, and indeed Europe's, strategic energy. This is not least because Britain remains an important player in the region for both historical and strategic reasons, and because Britain remains a major investor in the region and still retains some influence. Vitally, the British Sovereign Base Area on Cyprus overlooks much of the Middle East, something that has not been lost on the Russians. Indeed, without over-stating Britain's ability to influence the Middle East British expertise could prove invaluable across a region the security of which is intimately bound to that of Europe and the British base on Cyprus is a source of vital British strategic influence.

The Middle Eastern Transition Clock

What balance must Britain seek to strike between values and interests in the Middle East and how best to influence desired outcomes therein? Libya, Egypt, Iran, Iraq and Syria all-too clearly demonstrate again this inherent dilemma for British strategy. The scale of the challenge the Middle East poses British strategy is enormous. Imagine a twelve hour clock face on which midnight represents chaos and midday stability. Sadly, much of the Middle East today exists somewhere between one minute past midnight and three o'clock in the morning – no later and thus no more stable.

The United States Institute for Peace (USIP) and the US Army Peacekeeping and Stability Operations Institute (USPSOI) established five principles for effective transition from conflict to sustainable peace that in effect move time forward. These principles can be thus summarised: a safe and secure environment; rule of law; stable governance; sustainable economy; and social well-being. [67]

Take Libya and Iran. The 2011 collapse of the Gadhafi regime in Libya demonstrated the challenges of rescuing a failed state and some of the policy and strategy choices Britain must make across the Middle East. Indeed, taken together with Afghanistan, Iraq and Libya have in some ways become the litmus tests for effective engagement across much of the region, even if the political future of both Baghdad and Tripoli remain profoundly uncertain. British strategy is made infinitely more difficult by the often partisan position of the US in dealing with the Israeli-Palestinian conflict, which drives much grievance across the Middle East, and reinforces the diplomatic challenge faced by the EU and its member-states.

USIP defines a safe and secure environment as the "ability of the people to conduct their daily lives without fear of systematic or large-scale violence."[68] With so many militias across the country, and in effect two governments one in Tripoli and the other in Benghazi, it is going to be some time before a legitimate state monopoly over the means of violence is reasserted, or control over borders re-established. Critical to the entire transition process will be the extent to which Tripoli can weld the militias and the many tribes and groups they represent into a single national army. In Iraq the situation is even worse with ISIS making progress against both the Iraqi National Army and the Kurdish Peshmerga Baghdad's already weak fiat across much of Iraq is steadily collapsing. Equally, the February 2014 murder of Egyptian Coptic Christians in Libya demonstrated the reach of ISIS and its capacity to spread.

---

[67] See United States Institute for Peace (2009) "Guiding Principles for Stabilization and Reconstruction", (Washington: USIP & United States Army Peacekeeping and Stabilization Operations Institute).
[68] Ibidem p. 6-38.

Therefore, on the twelve-hour clock face, both Iraq and Libya are at best at 1 o'clock.

Rule of law is defined by USIP as the "ability of the people to have equal access to just laws and a trusted system of justice that holds all persons accountable, protects their human rights and ensures their safety and security."[69] A just legal framework for either Iraq or Libya will not only take time, but will prove an intensely political process. Islamist groups insist on a strict interpretation of Sharia law, which others find quite unacceptable. Indeed, the expulsion and murder of Christians in the Iraqi city of Mosul is indicative of the collapse of state order. Public order, another key facet of rule of law, is fragmented and uncertain. Logically, if the Middle Eastern state is to be saved the first order principle is to establish the unbiased rule of national law and then expand government writ across countries once the seat of government has been firmly re-established.

Be it Baghdad or Tripoli the realisation of such a goal is at present almost impossible to imagine. Indeed, accountability under the law, access to justice, and eventually a culture of lawfulness would require the establishment of an entirely new system for the administration of justice. Again, Iraq and Libya are not even at 1 o'clock on the transition clock.

Stable governance is defined as the "ability of the people to share access or compete for power through non-violent political processes and to enjoy the collective benefits and services of the state."[70] Iraq and Libya remain in the midst of conflict and post-conflict transition seems an increasingly distant prospect. Tripoli is only taking the first and most tentative steps toward representative government. Baghdad faces a growing Sunni-led insurgency generated in no small part by Shia sectarianism. Furthermore, both countries must cope with a hybrid political structure of secular, tribal and Islamist elements, all three of which are vying for supreme authority. The extent to which this equilibrium can be institutionalised with checks

---

[69] Ibidem p. 7-64
[70] Ibidem p 8-98

and balances to ensure that no single group dominates will be a critical test of transition.

A sustainable economy is defined by USIP as the "ability of the people to pursue opportunities for livelihoods within a system of economic governance bound by law."[71] According to the UN Development Programme Human Development Index, Libya is ranked 64th out of 186 states and Iraq 131st.[72] Equally, Libya enjoys a relatively educated population with enough of a middle class to, in principle at least, provide an entrepreneurial impetus to the economy. However, as *The Economist* of 9 January, 2015 states, "Nowadays, Libya is hardly a country at all. The factions that came together to fell Muammar Qaddafi have given up trying to settle their differences by negotiation…Libya has two rival governments, two parliaments, two sets of competing claims to run the central bank and the national oil company, no functioning national police or army, and an array of militias that terrorise the 6m citizens, plunder what remains of the country's wealth, ruin what is left of its infrastructure, and torture and kill wherever they are in the ascendancy".[73]

One of the first order requirements for any government is to re-establish macro-economic stability in areas such as consumer price inflation, grow the gross domestic product over one or more business cycles, promote positive change in measured unemployment and employment, ensure the effective management of fluctuations in government finances, and currency stability. Britain could certainly help that process but only when some semblance of order and governance has been re-established. However, neither Baghdad nor Tripoli control any real instruments over their conflict-torn economies and are thus incapable of establishing the functioning structures critical for effective economic governance. For that reason Iraq and Libya are no further forward than 1 o'clock.

---

[71] Ibidem p 9-132
[72] See http://hdr.undp.org/en/statistics/hdi
[73] "Libya: The Next Failed State", The Economist, 9 January, 2015

Social well-being is defined as the "ability of the people to be free from want of basic needs and to coexist peacefully in communities with opportunities for advancement."[74] Iraqi and Libyan high-grade hydrocarbon and gas reserves could, in time, fund the resources for meeting the basic needs of the people, but only in time. Indeed, at present ISIS is syphoning off a significant part of Iraq's oil to pay for its super-insurgency across the Levant and Mesopotamia. Tripoli moved to establish new contracts with potential partners, but lacks the necessary control to enforce or uphold such contracts.

At an estimated 41.5 billion barrels, Libya has the largest proven oil reserves in Africa—about 3 per cent of the global total—with much of the country unexplored due to past sanctions. The geology, however, looks very promising and even without further discoveries, Libya has some 20 years of reserves at 2009 production rates and its oil is also relatively easy to recover. In addition, the country has proven gas reserves of 52 trillion cubic feet, making it the world's 14th largest producer.[75]

Whilst Libya is probably ahead of Iraq on the transition clock, it is only at best at 2 o'clock. And with Tripoli only some 294 kms/184 miles from both the EU and NATO, Libya in particular is an immediate risk to British security. As for Iraq the future looks dark at best.

The Syria Debacle

Syria presents another immediate test for British strategy and a risk to British security. In the wake of Assad's use of chemical weapons on opposition civilians on 29 August 2013 Parliament voted to deny Prime Minister Cameron the right use force against the Assad regime. This highlighted the extent to which Syria presents Britain with a dilemma as London struggles with the value-interest in the face of an internal political struggle of a weak state that is creating a

---

[74] Ibidem –p 10-162
[75] See "FACTBOX – key facts about Libya's gas sector", Reuters http://uk.reuters.com/article/2007/05/29/uk-libya-gas-factbox-idUKL297607920670529

massive humanitarian crisis and fuelling a super-insurgency with very profound strategic implications, not least for Britain.

The crisis also serves to demonstrate how little Britain's leaders understand the implications of the Syria debacle. Indeed, Syria highlights a conflict inherent to British strategy. Hard though it is to accept given the nature of the current Damascus regime the preservation of the Syrian state in some form is an essential British interest. The Syrian civil war is not simply about the transfer of power from a minority to a majority, it is about the future geopolitical shape of the Middle East.

However, for Syria to find true peace new political coherence will need to be forged that reflects a Syria very different to that of 1966, when Assad's father seized power. That will not be easy. Syria is 90% Arab, with some two million Kurds plus other smaller groups making up the balance of a 22 million population that has exploded by over 300% since 1966. Syria is also 87% Muslim, with Shias making up 13% of the population as against 74% Sunnis, with the rest of the population comprised of small Christian, Druze and other communities. In the past, the Baathist constitution protected minorities. That is now gone swept aside by a brutal regime in Damascus and ISIS.

"The enemies of the people are the enemies of God, and the enemies of God will burn in hell." The words of Syrian President Assad at the launch of his January 2013 'peace' initiative left little grounds for optimism. Indeed, whilst the so-called Geneva Plan established the foundation for a resolution of the conflict it is extremely unlikely any 'big deal' can now be reached between Damascus, and in any case ever-more-marginalised Syrian National Coalition (SNC). However unpalatable it may be 'strategy' would suggest it may indeed be necessary to deal with either the existing regime or contemplate a fundamentalist entity in Damascus, with all that would entail for regional, and indeed European security.

And then there is ISIS. The fundamentalist Sunni fighters of ISIS are what Prime Minister David Cameron described as a "new cohort of al-Qaeda linked extremists", even though ISIS is so extreme as to have been effectively disowned by al-Qaeda.[76] If the Assad regime simply implodes doubtless a new struggle for power will begin, forcing Britain to consider carefully the outcomes it seeks. An Iran-friendly Assad regime or a fundamentalist Sunni Islamist government would profoundly and adversely affect the regional strategic balance.

How could Britain best apply its efforts? It is hard to say, although the effort must be firmly-embedded in the EU (the UN is blocked by Russia) and in harness with the US, and involve the sustained application of both soft and hard power. Experience of political transition in Afghanistan, Iraq and Libya would suggest that once a ceasefire is in place, all parties to the conflict would need to begin efforts at political reconciliation. Reprisal killings would need to be prevented and humanitarian suffering alleviated, with a new seat of government in Damascus rapidly established and protected. A clear political timetable for transition would also need to be crafted, allied to early disarmament, reconciliation and the rehabilitation of combatants.

To such an end, Syria's armed forces would need to be re-oriented, and essential services and the judicial system preserved to provide stability in transition. Assuming for a moment the eventual collapse of the Assad regime senior members would need to be charged under law and seen to receive a fair trial. National elections would also need to take place after the drafting of an interim constitution that would almost certainly need the inclusion of Baathists in the opposition, who would have been disarmed and effectively forced to choose between reconciliation and exclusion. In short Syria would need to be governed by the international community for a very long time and that is as unlikely to be acceptable to any Syrian, as it would be to many Britons tired of seemingly endless and unsuccessful foreign entanglements.

Furthermore, a Syrian peace cannot be detached from wider regional *Realpolitik*. Indeed, the conflict is very much part of that equation.

---

[76] See "David Cameron: Syria empowering new al-Qaeda generation", BBC News, 17 December, 2012, http://www.bbc.co.uk/news/uk-politics-20762098

Whilst an arms embargo has been formally-imposed evidence abounds that the embargo exists in name only. Iran has been supporting Damascus with both expertise and munitions, with substantial evidence existing of direct involvement of the Iranian Revolutionary Guard with Russia and China acting as cheerleaders. Indeed, the regional strategic ambitions of Iran and its proxy Hezbollah in its conflict with Israel have critically exacerbated the war. Equally, the Free Syrian Army (FSA) has been receiving, directly or indirectly, both small arms and man-held anti-aircraft missiles from the Gulf States and Saudi Arabia mainly to counter the regime's use of air power. The February 2015 decision by the Assad regime to suspend air attacks suggests that the door may be opening for some form of de facto alliance between Assad and the FSA against ISIS. However, peace remains a distant prospect.

Indeed, Britain can expect no peace soon, but as long as the conflict continues the threat to Britain's security will remain very real. Indeed, an enduring Syrian peace would only be possible with the consistent support of a unified international community and that simply does not exist. Even if it did is any state prepared to commit land forces under UN mandate to secure the peace and offer the large resources vital to re-settle peaceably an entire displaced population and thereafter promote peaceful transition? If Iraq and Libya are at 1 o'clock in the transition cycle Syria's clock is not even running.

UN Peace Envoy Lakhdar Brahimi is right. If Syria cannot be saved, what is left of it will be a danger to itself and its neighbours in what is already a very dangerous region. Saving Syria will not be easy but it is vital and not just for Syria because the conflict is really about the future of the entire Middle East and will demand of Britain and its allies an investment in time, money, and possibly even blood.

Egypt: The Crumbling Cornerstone of the Middle East

Egypt highlights the essential paralysis of British policy in the Middle East. London like so many Western capitals is simply waiting until either the situation improves or gets so dangerous that action becomes necessary, although what such action would entail is again hard to discern. After flirting with democracy in the Middle

East during the 2003 Iraq War when the Americans actively tried to impose it, Britain is again reconciling itself to the fact that democracy worthy of the name will be a long-time coming across much of the Arab world.

The fate of Egypt is in many ways a bell-weather and could well presage the fate of the wider Middle East, not least because one in four Arabs is Egyptian. The 2013 forced removal of President Morsi and his replacement by President al-Sisi opens a very uncomfortable question for those in Britain who believe democracy is a means to a stability end. It also raises several further questions about British strategy and the value-interest. In a master-class of under-stated British diplomatic fudgery former Foreign Secretary William Hague said of the Egyptian Army's 2013 'soft coup', "It's happened, so we will have to recognise the situation and move on".[77]

The 2013 military coup also demonstrated again what happens to British strategy when values and interests become conflated and the boundary between them ill-defined. Given the instability across the rest of the Middle East the seizure of power by General al-Sisi was clearly of strategic convenience to the West. And yet such power grabs are contrary to British values. The Muslim Brotherhood and President Morsi was elected to office with 52% of the popular vote and passed a constitution with the support of 62% of the electorate and 70% of a conservative Egyptian population ascribe to some form of Islamism. And, although there is clear evidence that former President Morsi was resorting to 'majoritarianism', i.e. ruling (not governing) in favour of those who supported him and not the country as a whole, he remains the only legitimately elected president in Egypt's history.[78]

---

[77] "William Hague says Britain does not support Egypt's military intervention and coup was a dangerous thing". Mail Online, 5 July, 2013. http://www.dailymail.co.uk/news/article-2356534/William-Hague-says-Britain-does-not-support-Egypts-military-intervention-and-coup-was-a-dangerous-thing.html

[78] Egypt is an object lesson in British influence. It was a fully autonomous part of the Ottoman Empire until 1882 when it became part of Britain's sphere of influence, the Suez Canal being a critical artery to Britain's eastern empire. With the defeat of the Turks by General Allenby Egypt became a British protectorate in

Sustainable democracy can only flourish when a) the majority of the people across the political spectrum share a sufficient commonality of values; and b) all the political parties that represent them are prepared to live by democratic rules. In Egypt, neither of those pre-conditions for stable democracy exists. There is no apparent common ground between the Islamists of the Muslim Brotherhood and the many secularists and others who occupied Cairo's Tahrir Square and who now ironically see the Egyptian Army as their political saviours. In other words, Egyptian democracy will take time.

So, where does Egypt go next? There is a curious political phenomenon in the Middle East. In those Arab states experimenting with democracy, almost everywhere anarchy is close to breaking out or killing people in large numbers, whereas those Arab states that have retained a monarchy are for the moment relatively stable.

How does this apply to Egypt? The first order principle for Britain is to put aside scruples about perfect democracy and work with those in power to stabilise the situation. Specifically, that means Britain and others helping the process of political transition towards enduring political institutions, a free press and an independent judiciary. Nor is Egypt Syria, even if experience of the past few years would suggest that unless the West pulls what levers it has (and even if it does) Egypt could also descend into sustained violence.

Therefore, instead of investing in the recreation of another 'democratic' version of a Nasser, Sadat or Mubarak in President al-Sisi, the strong man who becomes part of the problem, political transition (and support for) Britain should focus on making the Egyptian Parliament the centre of political gravity with checks and balances written into a new constitution. This would prevent one part of the population tyrannizing another, which is the essential dilemma in many Middle Eastern societies. Parliaments have rules

---

1915. The Sultanate that had ruled Egypt since the sixteenth century struggled on until overthrown by General Nasser in 1952. Since then Egypt has had a succession of Army generals in charge...and still has.

for democratic engagement and those that flout those rules can be sanctioned as in any other parliamentary democracy. Here, Britain and the EU could play a pivotal role.

Strategic Iran

What relationship should Britain seek with Iran? Iran aims to become the regional-strategic power in the Middle East and is in many ways a litmus test challenge for British strategy in the region. Whilst the November 2013 *Five plus One* talks between the five Permanent Members of the UN Security Council (Britain, China, France, Russia and the US) plus Germany and Iran on Tehran's nuclear ambitions pointed to a possible thawing of relations between Iran and the West, there is no reason to believe Tehran has tempered its regional-strategic ambitions. Moreover, Tehran's attempt to obtain nuclear weapons and advanced missile delivery systems is symptomatic of the age into which the world is moving. Fuelled by a mixture of regional power ambitions, oil revenue, a relatively weak state and the spread of destructive technologies, Iran's nuclear programme reflects Tehran's search for stability, prestige and influence at one and the same time. Iran's essential vulnerability is generated by its location and culture; a Shia Persian state in a largely Sunni Arab neighbourhood.

For that reason Iran exploits Israel as the enemy of choice to establish its Islamic credentials across much of the Arab world. Consequently, a critical Iranian need is to offset overwhelming Israeli conventional and nuclear military power through the use of proxy terror groups such as Hezbollah in Lebanon. Whilst the immediacy of the threat posed by Iran to the West has probably been over-stated, the challenge that such emerging and yet antagonistic powers pose cannot be over-looked. At the very least, the US and Britain must maintain pressure to constrain Iranian efforts to develop nuclear weapons. The November 2013 interim agreement was thus part of an attempt to establish a reward/punishment strategy that grants Iran benefits when it complies with nuclear prohibitions, and punishes Tehran when it moves forward with its nuclear ambitions.

On the face of it the interim agreement, if it is ever properly confirmed and assured (a big if), could be one of those moments in geopolitics which re-order security, certainly in the region. For its part Iran has agreed to slow efforts to enrich uranium to weapons-grade in return for the relief of some $7bn worth of sanctions. With inflation running at around 40% per annum in Iran and the regime under growing domestic pressure Tehran clearly has a need to end its domestic isolation. However, if the interim agreement is indeed to be confirmed, and President Obama in August 2014 agreed to its extension in the absence of a permanent agreement, any final treaty will need to pass two verifiable tests. Does the agreement reflect a fundamental shift in Iran's foreign and security policy posture? Is the Middle East made safer (and by extension the wider world) by such a treaty?

In return for the easing of sanctions Iran has agreed to give International Atomic Energy Authority (IAEA) inspectors daily access to the Natanz and Fordo nuclear sites, although Iran has clearly not abandoned its ambitions. In November 2014 Iranian Foreign Minister Mohammed Javad Zarif tweeted (a sign of the times?) that under the 1968 Nuclear Non-Proliferation Treaty (NPT), Iran has an "inalienable" right to enrich uranium. Technically, the Foreign Minister is correct, as a state may indeed enrich uranium up to 5% beyond which it is deemed weapons research has commenced.

Does the agreement reflect a fundamental shift in Iran's foreign and security policy posture? Critically, the test of Iran's *bona fides* will not simply be its adherence to any treaty, but whether Tehran's regional strategy also shifts. That would mean a markedly less hostile posture towards Israel, including less support for Hezbollah in Lebanon, less interference in the Syrian civil war (and other neighbouring states) and less interference in the Gulf. As yet there are no signs of such a shift. Rather, President Obama seems to be gambling that this agreement could bolster President Rouhani and the so-called 'moderates' in the Tehran regime, and that in time sufficient confidence can be established in Tehran to begin to shift Iran's essentially anti-Israeli, and by extension anti-American and anti-British strategy.

Is the Middle East made safer (and by extension the world) by a permanent treaty? That depends. Both Israel and Saudi Arabia have condemned this agreement. Israeli Prime Minister Netanyahu called it an "historic mistake" and that Israel reserves the right to defend itself. Immediately after the signing of the interim agreement in Geneva the leaders of several Gulf States flew to Riyadh for talks with the Saudi leadership, which has also privately condemned this agreement.

Critically, if Iran is not seen to observe, and more importantly held to observe, the final treaty then Saudi Arabia could well take forward already advanced talks with Pakistan for the development of nuclear weapons. To mix metaphors, if that happened then the nuclear genie would be well and truly out of the bottle and the Non-Proliferation Treaty (NPT) would be a busted arms control flush.

So, is a permanent treaty worth the strategic risk? Yes, but. Yes, in that any attempt to break the deadlock with Iran could if successful help eventually lead to an agreement between the Israelis and the Palestinians that is the source conflict in the Middle East.

Therefore, for all the justifiable hype about the interim agreement and a possible permanent treaty, British strategy should really be focussed on Iran's wider ambitions across the region. Iran like North Korea and Pakistan, sits at the crossroads of state competition, radicalism and emerging power. Whilst the "Global Zero" sought by the Obama regime to rid the world of nuclear weapons is of course desirable, it is also impracticable, and will almost certainly be impossible to realise.[79] The US is a status quo power and can afford to some extent such strategic largesse. However, states that are weak are unlikely to give up nuclear weapons. North Korea is a

---

[79] There are some very serious people close to the Obama Administration who believe that global nuclear disarmament is an achievable goal. Catherine McCardle Kelleher writes, "Present levels of nuclear armaments are viewed as "acceptable" and the risk of accident, miscalculation, or unauthorised use is "manageable". In this frame, however, the policy dialogue on nuclear zero is significantly impoverished". McCardle Kelleher, Catherine and Reppy, Judith (ed.) (2013) "Getting to Zero: The Path to Nuclear Disarmament" (Stanford: Stanford University Press) p 7.

case-in-point precisely because it is weak state. Moreover, Iran continues to promote Shia radicalisation across the region precisely because Tehran is insecure. Indeed, part-state, part Islamic theocracy Iran is accelerating the forced retreat of failing states built along Western lines in the face of a fundamentalist alternative whilst accelerating a possible future showdown of the fundamentalisms between Sunni and Shia.

Can the Middle Eastern State be Rescued?

Can the Middle Eastern state be rescued and what role should Britain play? Ever since the May 1916 Sykes-Picot accord carved up the Middle East into states under either British or French 'protection', the 'state' has often been seen as emblematic of both the Western system of governance and often corrupt government across much of the Islamic world. Therefore, the challenge for the British will be to help rescue the state as the natural focus for identity and provider of security in the eyes of many of those whom the state has failed in a region that could undergo a profound political transformation over the next decade. That is why an emphasis on 'upstream' conflict prevention and properly focussed aid and development policies are important parts of British national strategy. Indeed, a very real danger exists that the failure of states in the Islamic world could lead to the rapid collapse of the post-colonial order and the 'Balkanisation' of the Middle East into a form of Caliphate.

Sixty years ago many new states emerged from colonial administrations with new elites at the helm. Today, the post-colonial wave of optimism has given way to corruption with populations who regard their elites and indeed their states with deep suspicion. A former imperial power such as Britain must always be sensitive to the past but not haunted by it. Indeed, an opportunity now exists to help rescue the state not least because evidence would suggest the majority of people in failing states long for stability and reject extremism. One thing is clear; Britain can do very little in the Middle East alone.

Afghanistan: Irresolute Support?

What role should Britain play in a future Afghanistan? In 1842 Sir Charles Napier wrote perhaps the most succinct telegram in military history to mark his success at the end of the First Anglo-Afghan War - "Peccavi!" ("I have sinned").[80] It was a play on words; Napier had just conquered what is today the Pakistani province of Sindh.

The United States, Britain and its allies and partners failed in Afghanistan because they lacked sufficient strategic unity of effort and purpose and sufficient strategic patience to complete the mission. The consequential diminution in the standing of the West (and with it Britain) will be felt for years to come across the world, and in the reluctance of the British people to engage in such conflicts. The Armed Forces did their best, but they simply could not compensate for the strategic inadequacy of British leaders trying to fight a war on a peacetime footing. Moreover, *Operation Herrick* was consistently undermined by shifting political aims, weak strategy, woolly-thinking and in-fighting in London, a lack of forces and resources, together with a failure to properly integrate civilian and military efforts. Specifically, the shift from denying Al Qaeda Afghan territory to the eradication of the Poppy crop in the all-important Helmand Province simply proved beyond the British. As such, Afghanistan demonstrated all too clearly the inherent shallowness of contemporary British strategy.[81]

NATO is now engaged in the Operation Resolute Support mission that replaced the International Security Assistance Force (ISAF) when major combat operations ended in December 2014. Resolute Support is vital if Afghanistan is to have any chance of a future that is other than ghastly. In December 2014 President Obama reversed his position and re-committed some 10,000 American troops to support President Ashraf Ghani's Kabul regime, possibly out to

---

[80] http://www.historyextra.com/blog/sir-charles-napiers-sin
[81] On a visit to Afghanistan 15 December, 2013 Cameron suggested somewhat unfortunately "Mission accomplished". This echoed George W. Bush who in 2003 made the same announcement just as Iraq collapsed into a civil war-cum-insurgency.

2024. Indeed, without American backing Resolute Support will fail, a dark reality made all the more poignant by the August 2014 killing of US Major-General Harold Greene at the British-led Marshal Fahim National Defence University outside Kabul.

Afghanistan demonstrates all too clearly the cost of failed engagement and the extent to which failure has done much to accelerate Britain's political retreat from sound strategy. The cost was literal as much as figurative. For example, Afghanistan cost the US taxpayer around $110bn per year. It cost $1m simply to keep a single American soldier in Afghanistan for a year.[82] However, bereft of political will, the operation simply ran out of steam, which has critically undermined any public belief that the campaign was worth either the sacrifice or the huge investment, especially so given the endemic levels of corruption in the Afghan Government. The US says it will stay in Afghanistan now that President Ashraf Ghani and the Kabul Government has entered into "bilateral security arrangements" that offer American forces immunity from prosecution. This opens the way to a limited, but enduring training and mentoring mission.

What are the implications for the British? Either Britain retreats into a kind of twenty-first century fortress mentality, tries to 'do' Afghanistan 'better' elsewhere, or adapts strategy in light of the lessons-learned and experience-gained from some fourteen years of operations. At the very least SDSR 2015 must reflect on those lessons not least because Afghanistan could mark a strategic watershed.

There is certainly a very real danger that in the wake of the Afghanistan experience Britain (and to an extent the US) will either withdraw into a punish and strike strategy for all and any engagements, or retreat into a form of isolationism; expressing outrage at events but doing nothing whatever about the medium to long-term consequences for British security – a form of *Little Britain* that SDSR 2015 must help counter. Isolationism is a very real danger. In an 8 January, 2015 edition of the BBC TV programme

---

[82] "Ross Kemp in Afghanistan", DVD published March 2012.

"This Week" Labour MP Diane Abbott suggested that the British people had finally abandoned what she called "neo-imperial adventurism". She was in fact calling for isolationism, which would make Britain less not more secure.

Furthermore, for the first such time in NATO history Britain gave up the deputy commander slot for a major Alliance mission. Somewhat incredibly Germany and Italy offered to take the lead in Resolute Support in Britain's absence, having punched far below their respective weights for much of the campaign. In fact, Berlin and Rome are simply playing narrow politics and again demonstrates the tendency of all Europeans to play politics with strategy. Their *démarche* is more an attempt to mask their respective failures in Libya and Mali than make a real difference in Afghanistan. However, a precedent has been established by London that if not corrected will further undermine London's ability to influence a NATO that remains critical, not only to Britain's defence strategy, but wider national influence.

Certainly, the impact of Afghanistan on British strategic credibility has been sobering. What was missing throughout the Afghan Campaign was a political strategy, built on a regional strategy essential to peace in Afghanistan, and backed up by consistent unity of effort and purpose. Much of the blame must lie with Washington, but British irresolution meant opportunities were undoubtedly missed and British diplomacy in the region should have been far more effective. For example, the Taliban is by no means a monolithic entity as it contains many elements, from those wanting to protest against corrupt government, warlords to sheer opportunists who back the Taliban only in the short-term, but have no intention of accepting their hard-line religious creed. And, post-2014 Afghanistan will still need to be properly engaged if the strategic goal of denying an ungoverned space to Al Qaeda and its affiliates is to be fulfilled and sustained.

In the wake of ISAF a desperate race is now on to establish credible Afghan National Security Forces (ANSF) prior to the planned end of Resolute Support in late 2016. However, whilst the Afghan National Army (ANA) has made some real progress the force still neither looks nor acts like a modern army. Without training, mentoring and, above all credible air power there are real questions as to whether the ANA will stand and fight in the coming struggle. In other words, stabilising Afghanistan will take years and will need London to continue to engage at a time when both Britain's leaders and its people are sliding into isolationism.

Afghanistan has demonstrated again the difficulty British leaders find in making hard-headed policy and strategy and then staying the strategic course. The British have been in Afghanistan since late 2001 because engagement was perceived as the most effective and cost-effective way to to remain close to Washington and to prevent Al Qaeda using the Afghan (and Pakistani) space as a base for attacks on Britain. However, as time passed and the campaign become more difficult the British lost sight of the strategy and instead became too attached to the tactical - their little bit of Afghanistan in Helmand Province – as action therein became an end in itself.

Consequently, the implementation of strategy became detached from strategy itself. The challenge now is to create new strategy able to engage an Al Qaeda franchise that is as exportable as it is adaptable, and then pursue such strategy ruthlessly. Events in Algeria, Iraq, Libya, Syria and Yemen in 2014 suggest that Al Qaeda, ISIS and their like are by no means yesterday's threat. Al Qaeda will doubtless re-group on the Afghanistan-Pakistan border as the US and UK withdraw combat forces from Afghanistan.[83] How is anti-Al Qaeda strategy going to be adjusted? Or, with the abandonment of Helmand, is Britain effectively disengaging from a proactive anti-Al Qaeda strategy and retreating into a purely defensive posture

---

[83] Katherine C. Gorka and Patrick Sookhdeo are in no doubts about the threat still posed by Al Qaeda. "We must recommit ourselves to attacking this deadliest of enemies at the level which it deserves to be, which is the strategic. Osama bin Laden may be dead, but his ideology of global supremacy through religious war is more vibrant and appealing to audiences around the world that it was on the day before the attacks [on New York and Washington] more than a decade ago". See Gorka, Katharine C. & Sookhdeo, Patrick (2013) "Fighting the Ideological War: Winning Strategies from Communism to Islam" (Washington: Isaac) p 203.

allowing the enemy the choice of when and how to strike? These are strategic questions London still has to answer.

Indeed, in spite of attempts to engage moderate Islam there is still no long-term, coherent strategy against Islamic fundamentalism or non-violent extremism, either at home or abroad. Nor indeed is there any realistic effort to ensure the longevity of the post-2014 Afghan Government. Instead, Britain, like its allies, has retreated into the measurement of inputs to mask the failure of outcomes. Sadly, the failures in both Afghanistan and Iraq have also prompted a profound and dangerous shift in British strategy from engagement to disengagement, apparently in the hope that Britain can avoid the kind of Al Qaeda-inspired carnage unleashed on the London transport system in July 2005[84]

If Napier were alive today he would send London an entirely different and far less succinct telegram to the one he sent from Sindh. He would remind his political masters just why sacrifice was necessary in Afghanistan. "Stamus contra malo" - "We stand against evil". If that is not the case then why did Britain go to Afghanistan in the first place? As for the cost, what will be the cost of complete and utter failure?

The Democratisation of Mass Disruption

The world is about to enter a new nuclear age that could in turn inform a new concept of terror. Whilst the Nuclear Non-Proliferation Treaty (NNPT) remains a cornerstone of arms control, the likelihood of states that seek to challenge the West by gaining access to such technology grows with each passing year. Indeed, it is very hard to see how such aging and dangerous technologies can be kept out of the hands of such states, possibly even non-state actors.[85]

---

[84] On the morning of 7 July, 2005 four Islamist suicide bombers attacked the London public transport network. 52 people were killed with a further 770 injured. See BBC News "7 July Bombings". http://news.bbc.co.uk/2/shared/spl/hi/uk/05/london_blasts/what_happened/html/
[85] The Economist of 22 June , 2013 wrote, "British and American intelligence sources think it [Iran] is about a year away from having enough fissile material to

The early twenty-first century differs from any epoch since the 1648 Treaty of Westphalia established the modern European state system at the end of the Thirty Years War because of the potential that exists for the loss of state monopoly over mass destruction. Nuclear, chemical and biological destructive technology is now over seventy years old, with modern chemical weapons one hundred years old. Only time will tell if Britain's intelligence and security services will be able to get a grip of such groups, but it is vital they do. At present, the best that can be said is that the British security services are playing a dangerous game of catch-up that has been made no easier by the disruption caused by the public release of data stolen by former NSA contractor Edward Snowden. At the very least, the emergence of such threats demands a re-ordering of the assumptions and principles of security.

What is different today? The information superhighway and the cyber domain afford hostile states and groups, a new transnational identity, and an ability to gain access in principle to mass-disruptive and perhaps destructive technologies. Another paradox is that whilst the Internet is a foundation upon which the modern British economy is built it also enables terrorist planning, provides them with an ability to hide and moves the financial resources upon which they thrive. And, as the December 2014 hack of Sony Pictures by North Korea attests, such attacks can cause both political mischief and potentially strategic harm. It is a domain that Islamists are beginning to exploit in their open war with open societies.

The only way to counter such threats is to create much greater synergies between all state tools and develop counter-capabilities. At the very least, there needs to be much closer co-operation between military Intelligence and criminal intelligence, policing must become more joined up and intelligent (possibly requiring the

---

make a bomb and a further still from mastering the technologies to make a nuclear warhead small enough to fit onto one of its Shabab-3 ballistic missiles and carry out the tests needed to be confident the system works". See The Economist, "Breakout Beckons", p 21.

106

creation of a national police force), and armed forces must be given the capacity to move rapidly to interdict such threats as they emerge.

Furthermore, in the face of such threats whilst the balance between security and liberty must of course be maintained the security services must have the necessary power to interdict and prevent plots. However, such balance will only be struck by involving the British people and convincing them of the need for continued effort, vigilance and, of course, surveillance. Indeed, a strong partnership between the British state and its people will be essential. For too long the political culture has been one of keeping the people in a form of blissful ignorance about the nature and extent of the threat – that will need to change.

In essence, the democratisation of mass disruption poses a fundamental dilemma for a state like Britain. How can a state effectively and legitimately engage a non-state enemy that exists both within its borders and beyond and, at the same time, uphold the values that define liberal democracy? Edward Snowden's revelations seemed to have suggested falsely to many that the British State is as much a threat to civil liberties as Al Qaeda or the rapacious Chinese and Russian intelligence services. This is nonsense. Liberty and security is a very difficult balance for a modern liberal-democratic state to strike. Failure at one extreme creates the very conditions of intolerance such groups seek to exploit so that they can promulgate their message of hate. Failure at another extreme simply opens the door to carnage on Britain's streets.

In June 2013 Snowden alleged that the US National Security Agency (NSA) and Britain's Government Communications Headquarters (GCHQ) had developed a new computer programme called PRISM to tap into emails and websites. In fact, only 6000 work at GCHQ and they face a host of plots and potential attacks at any one time and, as the January 2015 Paris attacks demonstrated, the need to ensure security and preserve liberty is indeed a difficult balance to strike for any open society. On the face of it, there are more than enough legal and procedural safeguards to ensure the proper accountability under law of the security services. Sadly, confidence in the state has undoubtedly been damaged by the Snowden revelations and the only 'winners' are the terrorist and criminal networks committed to attacking Britain.

Therefore, confidence must be restored and quickly. The fusion of terrorism and the global flows of illegal-funding in support of such groups raises the very real spectre of terrorists armed with mass-destructive power, if not in the immediate future certainly in the none-too-distant future. Such a threat could act as an asymmetric leveller forcing states such as Britain to seek a balance between a credible defence against such groups and sufficient expeditionary military power to deter, disrupt and, if necessary, reach out and destroy. If that happens then counter-proliferation, counter-terrorism, counter-insurgency and counter-intelligence would need to be merged and Britain's security effort organised accordingly.

However, implicit in the 7/7 attacks in London and the January 2015 attack on French journalists in Paris, is the most profound of strategic questions that government must answer; fight or flight? Indeed, without a reasonably secure home base properly protected and defended, allied to a sufficiently robust society able and willing to engage in the consequence management of inevitable attack, the willingness of any British government to project power and influence will be drastically reduced. If that happens then far from helping to shape the twenty-first century strategic security agenda Britain will have decided to become a victim of it.

Competing in the Global Race

This brief survey of Britain's strategic environment reinforces the challenges the country faces and the need for an effective and agile national strategy built on alliances and partnerships and invested by real British power. Be it the threat posed by terrorism or states the relatively benign world-view in National Security Strategy 2010 is already out-dated, something made tragically clear by the attack on the Paris offices of *Charlie Hebdo* by Islamist terrorists on 7 January, 2015. There is a growing need for Britain to compete effectively in the global race with states such as China and Russia and against radical groups such as Al Qaeda and ISIS. This in turn suggests a new, truly strategic mind-set is needed in government from top to bottom together with a fundamental re-organisation of state tools and the proper investment and commitment of appropriate resources. Instead, faced with death and suffering on the nightly TV news many Britons may be inclined to pull up the drawbridge and seek 'security' in a kind of fortress mentality. That would be disaster for Britain and its people and Britain's leaders must resist it, whatever the opinion polls say.

Intelligence and knowledge will be critical weapons in this very twenty-first century fight. Equally, effective international institutions must remain central to British strategy. However, far from becoming stronger such institutions are becoming weaker and could in time fail if the world retreats into competing blocs that paralyse effective multilateral action.

Facing up to the challenges in Britain's strategic environment will stretch a London bureaucratic elite who are both exhausted and over-stretched and a political elite that is too often complacent, very often in denial and determined to focus on the politics of the moment rather than the strategy necessary for Britain's future security. However, whatever the challenge the world poses it is one British strategy must grip.

Equally, there can be no security in simplistic one-dimensional views of threat by focussing almost exclusively on terrorism, dangerous though that threat is. Paradoxically (and counter-intuitively), there is a danger that terrorism could become a kind of comfort zone which helps Britain's leaders avoid the emerging systemic challenges posed by the new geopolitics. In such circumstances, Britain would fail to properly consider the large ends of grand strategy in the round and the large means that would need to be devoted to the achievement of such ends in the coming years. Indeed, given the growing pressures in the international system 'threat' is not just about failed states and failed ideas. Good old-fashioned Realpolitik is back as Russia is demonstrating in Ukraine with its typically gruff strategic eloquence.

Furthermore, the list of risks and threats discussed herein is by no means complete. There are also tensions in the Arctic High North,

109

concerns over the security of the Gulf States, Baltic insecurity, conflict in the Horn of Africa, piracy, human and drug trafficking, trade insecurity, organised crime, frictions caused by a rapidly growing world population, and of course the seemingly intractable conflict between Israel and the Palestinians. The Israeli's 2014 offensive in Gaza demonstrated again just how far a peace settlement is from being agreed. The challenge for Britain and its allies and partners will be to see these challenges in the strategic round, not as a series of iterative one-offs, and yet devote appropriate and sufficient attention to each and every one of them.

Clearly, the scope, extent and nature of change is challenging traditional British concepts of security and defence and demanding creative approaches to conflict prevention, response and consequence management. It is change that will also demand of Britain's leaders a determination to influence events not merely to react to them. It is this challenge that British leaders schooled in politics rather than strategy will find perhaps the most challenging of all. Therefore, to meet that challenge London must think anew about British power and influence and to what ends they are applied and how. Partnership will, of course, be central to British strategy. However, such method will only be achieved if Britain has the power to be an attractive partner and sufficient societal and governmental cohesion to act as a leader.

Therefore, to compete effectively in the global race the British must first have a sound grasp of the scope and extent of change and a clear understanding about where best to focus British strategic effort. At the very least, Britain must re-develop a sound capacity to scan the strategic horizon, because only then will the British re-establish a proper appreciation of the extent and nature of the power shifts taking place in the world. And, only then can the fashioning of British security policy, from which national strategy flows, be properly made with any confidence. Such a response will need to be necessarily radical, rather than incremental and one really wonders if either Westminster or Whitehall are up to that so closed are they both (and so often) to new thinking. Indeed, any such proper appreciation of Britain's world will necessarily lead to a range of assumptions and policy choices that will re-fashion Britain's political, security, diplomatic and military effort into the future.

At the very least strategic clarity of thought is needed in London if Britain is to regenerate the power and prestige critical to influence. Therefore, British strategy must be dynamic and necessarily seek and promote change across the strategic environment with a clear aim to convince revisionist powers and forces in the world that engagement in the Western-inspired system of values and interests would be to their benefit. At the same time those forces irreconcilable to and with the West must be marginalised, contained, and if so required, destroyed.

However, to have any chance of shaping strategic events and the outcomes Britain must seek London must again become seen as a serious player in a big, strategic game. Today it is not. Such influence will not be easy to re-generate given London's loss of direction and momentum and the precipitous fall from power and prestige that has occurred in recent years. Indeed, Britain is dangerously close to being relegated from the world's power Premier League not because of the facts of power, but because of a lack of ambition, poor organisation, reduced investment, and weak leadership.

Therefore, given the complex environment into which Britain is moving successful security governance will demand a new relationship between the generation of sound strategy, its flexible and agile application and the necessary tools of power needed to convince others that Britain is powerful enough to prevail, most likely in league with others.

4.

Grand Strategy: Alliances, Partnerships and Institutions

"The manoeuvre which brings an ally into the field is as serviceable as that which wins a great battle. The manoeuvre which gains an important strategic point may be less valuable than that which placates or overawes a dangerous neutral".

Winston S. Churchill[86]

Britain has always conducted grand strategy as part of grand alliances, even at the height of the Victorian empire. Therefore, Britain must have the power to actively reinvest in the alliances, partnerships and institutions, which given Britain's world are central to British national strategy. That means a Britain itself armed with the necessary and requisite tools and instruments of influence to shape, manage and at times lead coalitions and alliances.

Institutions, Power and Partnerships

Alliances, partnerships and international institutions are the essential transmission mechanism between policy, strategy and effect in British grand strategy. And yet in 2015 Britain is moving towards a possible EU exit, losing influence over NATO and as marginal to US grand strategy as at any time since World War Two and the creation of the Special Relationship. This marginalisation is not simply due to London's beggar-thy-neighbour politics, even though narrow party politics has a lot to do with Britain's retreat from influence. Rather, it is more a function of London's retreat from the first principles of power politics. The language of power may have changed over the years, especially in the dialogue between the Western democracies, but international relations in any form is still essentially about power and the ability of a state to influence others. Moreover, whilst international institutions were created both to prevent extreme state behaviour and to aggregate legitimate state

---

[86] In Freedman, Lawrence (2013) "Strategy: A History" (Oxford: Oxford University Press) p.139

113

power they are still essentially built on the relative power that exists between their respective members. This is something that Britain and its political leaders seem to have forgotten.

There are four questions Britain must thus consider concerning the international institutions central to British strategy. What does Britain want institutions to do? What is the likely future strategic and future operating environment (FOE) in which institutions will function? What must Britain bring to the institutions to ensure their effectiveness? How can Britain best influence international institutions? The four questions further underpin two British strategic truisms; Britain's influence over international institutions is directly proportionate to the political, intellectual and actual capital Britain invests in them. Britain's political capital (soft power) can only be realised if supported by hard power that is seen by others (adversaries and allies) as credible and useable.

If Britain stays in the EU (and it is a big 'if' given the extent to which the Union has become a politically-paralysed, mutual impoverishment pact) London's first aim must be to keep security and defence firmly under national control, even if limited defence integration takes place between smaller EU member-states. However, to achieve such a goal given that non-Eurozone Britain is so marginal to an EU leadership that is focused almost exclusively on the Eurozone, will demand of the British a military force that is unequivocally Europe's leader and thus most powerful. Moreover, only by confirming Britain's position as Europe's strongest military power will London confirm NATO as the central institution for the security and defence of Europe, preserve American commitment to Europe and ensure British influence in and over Europe commensurate with the national interest. Such influence also pre-supposes a new political settlement between Eurozone and non-Eurozone member-states of the EU, the latter group which Britain should aspire to lead.

It is hard to over-state the damage Britain's 2010 defence cuts did to the international institutions central to British strategy, and Britain's influence over them. Indeed, too often British governments have seen institutions as compensation for national cuts to armed forces and/or diplomatic means. Instead, British governments must see international institutions such as the EU or NATO for what they or at least should be; strategy and influence-multipliers. In other words, if London is to generate cost-effective strategic influence and effect via institutions Britain must invest those institutions with real power. The need is pressing as the three most important institutions for Britain - EU, NATO and UN - are all in deep trouble in one way or another.

Furthermore, within the context of institutional security there are three axes of influence that British strategy must pursue. First, Britain must remind European partners that there are others with whom Britain can act. Second, the British must remind allies and partners that membership of either the EU or NATO is a contract in which British support for the security of allies and partners must be matched in return by allied/partner support for Britain's own security. Third, Britain must actively seek to influence new partners by using institutions as frameworks for strategic relationships that possess a clear commitment to the just and effective application of both coercive and non-coercive security policy the world over.

Britain and the United Nations

Central to British strategy must be the maintenance of Britain's status as a Permanent Member of the United Nations Security Council (UNSC) because of the influence such membership generates for Britain. Indeed, even though the UN itself is dysfunctional it remains the world's supreme international political authority. Some states question Britain's right to a permanent member seat citing relative population size or other criteria. They suggest the UNSC reflects the world of 1945, rather than 2015. In fact, the UNSC is not an executive committee of the United Nations, but rather a security council upon which only the world's most capable military powers hold permanent seats. For now Britain remains one of the world's top five real military powers, although with the British fast slipping down the league table of military power London's ability to defend the right of permanent membership will inevitably come under more pressure. Therefore, precisely because Britain's armed forces are the currency for UNSC permanent membership London must consciously and purposively maintain Britain as a top five world military power. This is because permanent membership of the UNSC also reinforces the centrality of Britain at the heart of other influence networks, such as the G7/8 and G20, and is thus critical to British influence.

Britain and NATO

NATO is still configured for a past world which has been masked by over a decade of operations in Afghanistan that are now at an end. The September 2014 NATO Wales Summit, which was hosted by Prime Minister Cameron, began to consider the strategic future of the Alliance. However, the final declaration was so full of caveats that Wales was at best only a very tentative strategic reawakening. At the summit David Cameron committed Britain to maintaining defence spending at 2% GDP. However, according to Professor Malcolm Chalmers of RUSI defence spending will fall to 1.88% of GDP 2015-2016 and 1.56% GDP 2016-2017.[87] If such a gap between rhetoric and reality grows it will encourage other NATO members to similarly play fast and loose with defence facts and the defence pretence from which NATO suffers will worsen.

In fact, Britain needs a NATO 3.0; a new Alliance that builds on the 2010 NATO Strategic Concept and which is designed to re-establish a link between the strategic political and military mechanism that is NATO's purpose and the future strategic operating environment. In September 2014 Norway's former Prime Minister Jens Stoltenberg took over as NATO Secretary-General and today faces one of the greatest strategic challenges to the Alliance since the Cold War. The threat comes not specifically from Russia or ISIS, unpredictable and potentially dangerous though they are. The most pressing threat to the Alliance comes from the seemingly endless Eurozone crisis which is destroying European defence-investment as NATO members steadfastly refuse to invest in or modernise their armed forces.

---

[87] See Chalmers, Malcom (2014) "The Financial Context for the 2015 SDSR: The End of UK Exceptionalism?" Royal United Services Institute, London. September 2014.

In that light Britain's job as Europe's most capable military power will be to nudge European members of the Alliance back to strategic reality. At the very least, common senses would suggest that Britain's aim must be to restore credible military power as the hard bedrock upon which the twenty-first century influence and effect of a twenty-first century Atlantic Alliance must necessarily be built. Only four NATO members meet the Alliance defence-spending guideline and if one looks closely at the language of the Wales Summit Declaration, few have any appetite to meet that target for at least a decade. Or, to put it another way, most EU member-states have abandoned defence until the Eurozone crisis is fixed. And, in spite of the European Central Bank initiating quantitative easing (printing money) in late January 2015 there is still no end in sight to the crisis.

For NATO to succeed military agility will also be vital. That means an Alliance properly-equipped with modern, professional and deployable forces. NATO today is both coalition generator and commander for offensive security operations by assorted members and partners alike and an absolute defence guarantor for its members. To a limited extent the Wales Summit succeeded in reinforcing both missions. The Readiness Action Plan, the centrepiece of the Summit suggested a new agile strategy that in effect merges collective defence, crisis management and co-operative security into a coherent security and defence concept. The addition of cyber-defence to collective defence was certainly a step down the road to the eventual overhaul and modernisation of Alliance collective defence that is long overdue.

However, it is where ambition and investment meet that NATO's ambition really hits the buffers. Or, to put it another way, creating yet more acronyms from less forces does not meet the strategic challenge the Alliance faces. With a new Spearhead force designed to 'complement' the existing NATO Response Force and the seven High Readiness Forces at NATO's military core, one has to ask just how many such forces the Alliance can create from ever-shrinking militaries. Certainly, at the level of force structure the Wales Summit Declaration simply does not add up.

Reorganising (again) ever shrinking available forces into ever more forces makes no sense if such an effort simply adds more commitments. And yet new forces cost a lot of money and on the critical issue of defence spending the Summit Declaration simply demonstrates the extent to which the Eurozone crisis has (and is) undermining NATO. As the Summit Declaration states, "the **aim**", is "…to move towards the 2% **guideline** within a **decade with a view** to meeting their [nations] NATO Capability Targets and filling NATO's Capability shortfalls" [*author's emboldening*]. [88]

The Summit also pointed towards a two-speed NATO that will rarely if ever operate at 28. The news that a 'core coalition' of NATO allies (plus Australia) will join the US in combatting ISIS reinforces the idea of the Alliance as an organiser of US-led coalitions for those states that can and will act. The states involved are in and of themselves interesting - America, Australia, Britain, Canada, Denmark, France, Germany, Italy, Poland and Turkey. This is clearly a core group with whom the Americans will do business. Germany's presence is important and to be commended even if an October 2014 report by KPMG and lawyers Taylor Wessing, revealed the lamentable state of the German armed forces.

Naturally, the Summit had to clear up the usual unfinished business – the maintenance of an Open Door policy to new members, the need to remain engaged in Afghanistan post December 2014, the usual rhetoric about NATO-EU relations and the even more usual rhetoric about defence-industrial co-operation. Indeed, there was something of an 'overtaken by events', formulaic quality to these Declaration paragraphs which clearly suggests little political appetite to actively pursue such 'commitments'.

The big elephant in the Welsh room was of course Russia. The Summit Declaration used strong language, "We condemn in the strongest terms Russia's escalating and illegal military intervention

---

[88] "Wales Summit Declaration: Issued by the Heads of State and Government participating in the meeting of the North Atlantic Council in Wales". 5 September, 2014. www.NATO.int

in Ukraine and demand that Russia stop and withdraw its forces from inside Ukraine and along the Ukrainian border". [89] That said there was nothing in the Declaration to make President Putin blink and Moscow simply sees such language as NATO posturing after the Russian-imposed Ukrainian fact.

For all that, some progress was made in Wales and Prime Minister David Cameron can take some credit for that. Indeed, with strong American support the Summit was in the end something of a success for British diplomacy and London is to be congratulated for that. Cameron's confirmation at the Summit that the second of Britain's new super-carriers *HMS Prince of Wales* will join the Royal Navy as planned was good timing, decent politics and effective leadership. The same can also be said for Britain's offer to take the 2017 lead of the new Very High Joint Readiness Force agreed at the Summit by committing 1000 troops. However, if Britain is to continue to lead by example (a very big if) London must also maintain the commitment Cameron made at the Wales Summit to maintain British defence spending at above the 2% GDP target.

It is clear that NATO today has a very long way to go before the Alliance is in that now hackneyed phrase 'fit for purpose', for all the challenges that the world will undoubtedly throw at it. This is not least because NATO's own bureaucracy seems incapable of properly understanding the scale of the challenge the Alliance faces and will face. Britain must work hard with allies to remedy the increasingly dangerous other-worldliness of the Alliance, but will be unable to do so until its own defence house is in order.

Worse, for all its eloquence strategy-killing politics still oozes from the many pages of the NATO Wales Summit Declarations reflecting a fundamental and dangerously false assumption on the part of the British and other allies; that the United States is and will remain the strongest military power on the planet by some distance and for the foreseeable future. Yes, the Americans are still the strongest

---

[89] "Wales Summit Declaration: Issued by the Heads of State and Government participating in the meeting of the North Atlantic Council in Wales". 5 September, 2014. www.NATO.int

military power but the US military is facing defence *cuts* between now and 2020 greater than the combined defence *expenditure* of ALL the NATO Europeans.[90] In other words, the great age of unrivalled American military supremacy is fast coming to an end and NATO needs collectively to consider the strategic implications.

And yet, if NATO members could get their collective act together as part of a twenty-first century transatlantic security contract they could a) help keep the US strong where it needs to be strong – Eastern Europe, the Middle East and Asia-Pacific; and b) demonstrate to the world that whatever a state spends on armed force such expenditures will never outstrip those of the West and is thus a waste of money. To do that NATO and its members will need to look hard at how real efficiencies can be found and new strategic partnerships generated the world-over to multiply real strategic effectiveness. That will require a radical NATO with a radical Britain at its core and a London prepared to lead by defence example.

NATO's bottom-line is this; the United States is the only power that is present in strength in every world region. However, to be critically strong in every region the US will need NATO Allies that can act credibly in and around Europe as crisis first-responders with Britain to the fore. Succeed and NATO will reinvent itself as an Alliance and regenerate itself in the American political mind. Fail and NATO will simply fade into anachronistic strategic irrelevance and the world will be a very much more dangerous place for that. If NATO does fail then the cost of defending Britain will become very much greater.

In 1991 NATO leaders met to consider the implications of peace in Europe. In 2014 they met ostensibly to consider the profound and dangerous implications of the rapid shift in the global balance of power away from NATO member nations. London in 1991 set the future orientation of the Alliance right up to 9/11. In spite of the grand language about a Europe "whole, free and at peace" which set the course for NATO and EU enlargement there was an implicit

---

[90] Author's own research.

question in London that has come to define the Alliance ever since: how little can be spent on defence?

Through the Wars of the Yugoslav Succession in the 1990s, the Kosovo war, 911, Afghanistan, Libya and elsewhere, Europeans have been unwavering in their collective belief that whatever happens they will spend less on defence. Indeed, defence cuts have become a political dogma that was only strengthened by the 2008 financial crash and the Eurozone crisis and has helped drive Europe's retreat from strategic realism. It has also fostered the appeasement of reality and a "we only recognise as much threat as we can afford" culture amongst leaders that has so damaged the Alliance.

With Russia's hybrid war in Ukraine, the ISIS super-insurgency on NATO's strategic doorstep, Iran and its nuclear ambitions, the rapid rise of strategic China, proliferation of destructive technologies across the world and a range of other potential threats it is clear that such self-deluding dogma has to be challenged and the age of false defence premiums finally brought to an end. Indeed, with NATO leaving Afghanistan the twenty-first century Alliance finally began in Wales; the place where NATO properly and finally began to prepare for the global Cold Peace that is being inexorably-fashioned beyond Alliance borders in the battle between the West and the new forces of intolerance, illiberalism and expansionism. Thus, whilst the Summit was a limited success it only began to address the challenges that lie ahead.

The first casualty of the Cold Peace is the assumption that the Americans will always be able to defend Europe irrespective of Europe's own defence effort. Indeed, the central issue at the Wales Summit was implicitly the fashioning of a new twenty-first century transatlantic security contract founded on principles of political realism. However, for such a contract to work NATO Europe can no longer play at Alliance if the United States is to maintain credible influence in Asia, Europe and the Middle East. This implies that Europe's defence can only be assured in the first instance by Europeans able and capable of acting autonomously in and around Europe. Britain needs to be in the vanguard of any such effort. The

121

Wales Summit also implied the striking of a new balance between protection of societies and the projection of power. If that balance is indeed to be struck all security and defence tools from intelligence to armed force, civil and military, will need to be radically re-cast and re-fashioned to *prevent* conflicts upstream and *engage* in conflict if needs be when, where and how it happens.

Furthermore, the end of major combat operations in Afghanistan reveals a Britain (and thus a NATO) that is entering a new and unpredictable era as the Alliance shifts from campaigns and operations to strategic contingencies. The word 'strategic' is the key as it means 'big' and that implies ambition, forces, resources and a fundamental change of mind-set on the part of political leaders. Therefore, the Wales Summit in effect began NATO's (and by extension Britain's) search for the answer to five twenty-first century strategic questions concerning the full realisation of the 2010 NATO Strategic Concept and the three core tasks therein of collective defence, crisis management and co-operative security. Can NATO provide credible collective defence to its members? What level of reassurance can NATO provide to both members and partners, including the permanent stationing of Alliance forces in the Baltic States? What support can NATO realistically offer to states on its margins? What relationship should now be sought with an assertive Russia? What more can NATO allies do to support the US in its global mission and at the same time ensure and assure security and defence in and around Europe?

Unless Britain takes radical steps to re-generate its military power the Americans will find it ever harder to properly re-engage in NATO even if they want to. The extensive talk of a US 'pivot' or 'rebalancing' to Asia-Pacific suggests an element of choice. In fact Washington is being forced to focus relatively-declining military strength in Asia-Pacific. Therefore, in spite of Russia's annexation of Crimea and its use of hybrid warfare in Eastern Ukraine getting the US to re-engage in NATO will not prove easy in the wake of Afghanistan given American commitments elsewhere and growing political frustration in Washington.

There is however a deeper problem London must confront if it is to use reinvestment in military power as a way of convincing the US to again align its strategic interests with Britain and other European allies. The US attitude towards international institutions is and will remain the most striking example of the divergence that exists between American and British strategic cultures. For Washington institutions have always been seen as ways to constrain and organise other states behind American leadership rather than mechanisms for legitimate and effective action in and of their own right. In recent years, the failure of European allies to live up to their commitments to improve military capabilities at several NATO summits has deepened the cynicism about the value of the Alliance and indeed international institutions in Washington, particularly in the Pentagon.[91]

A militarily credible future Alliance rests upon the realisation of a credible and deployable force - NATO 2020. NATO 2020 is not just critical for the Alliance but also for Britain's future security and defence choices. The question though is (as ever); will the plan ever be realised? "NATO 2020: Assured Security: Dynamic Engagement" of 17 May, 2010 states: "Between now and 2020 it [NATO] will be tested by the emergence of new dangers, the many-sided demands of complex operations, and the challenge of organising itself efficiently in an era where rapid responses are vital, versatility critical and resources tight".[92]

In the wake of Wales Britain should promote NATO 2020 as a steady and consistent reform agenda for an Alliance that must be rendered fit for purpose for the twenty-first century, both as a regional-strategic hub for the generation and effective command and

---

[91] There is one very clear exception to this trend – Poland. "The Economist" states, "Having weathered the past five years better than most - the economy has grown by a fifth since 2009 – and imposed spending limits on most departments, the centre-right government of Donald Tusk, re-elected in 2011, has made modernising the armed forces a priority. This year's defence budget of $9.5bn has grown by 7% over 2012, bringing Poland close to the 2% of GDP target that all NATO members are supposed to meet, but very few do". See "Flexing its Muscles". "The Economist", 17 August, 2013 pp 21-22.
[92] See Lindley-French J. (2013) "Challenges to the Alliance Toward 2020", Italian Atlantic Committee, http://www.comitatoatlantico.it/en/studi/nato-2020-2/

control of coalitions, and as a cornerstone of global stability. Succeed and the Americans will be convinced and the Alliance and Britain will be more secure. Fail and Britain will not.

Twenty-first century collective defence will also require the modernisation of architectures to include advanced deployable forces, cyber-defence and resiliency, as well as missile defence. Britain has a vital role to play in leading the European allies through such modernisation primarily by leading by example. Critically, as events in the Middle East and Eastern Europe show the ability of the Alliance to conduct successful operations outside Alliance borders will also be vital. Finally, Britain must act quickly if the corporate memory gained in over a decade of operations in Afghanistan is not lost and cannot thus be incorporated in the modernisation and future best practice of Alliance forces.

Consultation mechanisms to prevent or manage crises effectively must also be improved and here Britain can again help take the lead. In many ways Article 4 of the North Atlantic Treaty has become the defining treaty instrument for the Alliance. However, without much greater unity of effort and purpose in the early phases of conflict, NATO will continue to be seen as an inadequate fire brigade, slow to act and incapable upon arrival. Such a perception will by extension badly undermine Britain's credibility as a strategic actor given the centrality of the Alliance to British strategy.

Innovation will be vital if the Alliance is to meet twenty-first century challenges and if London has the vision and the will to seize the moment Britain could be in the vanguard of Smart Defence. Former Secretary-General Anders Fogh Rasmussen said in a speech to the 2010 Chicago Summit that: "In these times of austerity, each euro, dollar or pound sterling counts. Smart defence is a new way of thinking about generating the modern defence capabilities the Alliance needs for the coming decade and beyond. It is a renewed culture of co-operation that encourages Allies to co-operate in developing, acquiring and maintaining military capabilities to undertake the Alliance's essential core tasks agreed in the new NATO strategic concept. That means pooling and sharing capabilities, setting priorities and co-ordinating efforts better".[93]

The challenge for Britain is that at the military level Smart Defence reflects a basic conceptual tension between American-led military transformation aimed at enhanced Allied capabilities and thus greater burden-sharing, and European force 'modernisation' which is aimed primarily at cutting armed forces as efficiently as possible. Britain needs to resolve that tension through leading by example.

Furthermore, if Britain is to properly exploit NATO, the Alliance must also be better able to exploit its two types of partnership – strategic partnerships and stability partnerships. Strategic partnerships are with states the world-over that can influence the strategic environment and stability partnerships are with regional partners the failure of which would endanger security and stability in and around Europe. One set of relationships concerns the need to aggregate and project power and influence, hence Britain's need to reinvest in the capability of its armed forces. The other set concerns effective defence diplomacy to preserve and renovate weak states, hence Britain's need for sufficient military capacity to assist in the training and reform of partner states. In 2015 this is most obviously needed in the re-training of Iraqi forces to fight ISIS.

However, the most pressing need is NATO's own military modernisation. Specifically, Britain must help lead the way in the development of new military capabilities that will promote real military transformation and reform in Europe. Indeed, perhaps the greatest threat to NATO's credibility is the European failure to match shrinking capabilities with growing commitments. Resolving this crisis will only be possible through the radical (and further) re-structuring of the NATO command structure. The British must also insist on an updated NATO nuclear weapons policy to render it fit for the coming new nuclear age and the growing need to re-establish a credible nuclear deterrent.

However, it is perhaps at the politico-military level that Britain needs to exert most influence and that means a renewed statement about Britain's commitment to real, twenty-first century British

---

[93] See "NATO-Smart Defence" www.nato.int/cps/en/natolive/78125.htm

military power and its place at the heart of the Alliance. Post-Afghanistan NATO will need to be transformed to act as a strategic hub. That is not to suggest NATO should seek a global role *per se,* but the Alliance must be open to partners outside of the Euro-Atlantic area who wish to align their armed forces with NATO practice and NATO standards. To that end, the Alliance must itself work much harder over the coming years to move beyond the rhetoric of interoperability and establish best practice for the generation and command of flexible coalitions. Britain clearly has a vital role to play in facilitating such relationships not least as some of the key partners are countries such as Australia with which Britain shares a very strong political and military heritage.

Britain, the EU and Critical European Partnerships

It had been hailed as THE EU European Defence Summit. Instead the December 2013 EU summit failed and revealed again the woeful inadequacy of the European defence effort. The active defence of Europeans by Europeans can only now be resolved by either structural increases in defence expenditure (unlikely but necessary) and/or much greater unity of strategic effort and purpose leading to deep defence synergy (necessary but unlikely). For some of the smaller NATO and EU members that will mean defence integration that begins in the tail but reaches towards the teeth-end of armed forces (desperate, necessary and yet still unlikely). Seventeen years on from the 1998 St Malo Declaration in which Britain and France gave new impetus to EU-led defence Britain must again seek common strategic cause with France, and with Germany.[94]

The relationship with France will also be vital in rendering NATO fit for purpose. However, for France to overcome its latent suspicions of NATO, Paris will expect deeper British political investment in CSDP. One aspect of that relationship will be British support for the

---

[94] The British-French Summit Declaration of 3-4 December, 1998 at St Malo stated, "...the [European] Union must have the capacity for autonomous military action, backed up by credible military forces, the means to decide the use them, and a readiness to do so, in order to respond to military crises". See "From St Malo to Nice – European Defence Core Docments" (2001) (Paris: WEU: ISS) p. 8

strengthening of the EU as a homeland security hub across the European security space. Indeed, if NATO is once again to become the strategic military sword and shield of the Euro-Atlantic Community, the EU would need to transform itself into a security hub, better able to provide civilian protection of the European homeland through improved and enhanced resiliency.

Furthermore, the EU must also be able to provide a credible political option for leaders so that European forces can be used effectively under a European flag when necessary. This would better enable political leaders to feel more confident in taking pro-active offensive action together when deemed necessary. Indeed, the flag a force operates under is almost as important as the force deployed in complex environments where politics and insecurity are one and the same.

However, all of the above pre-supposes a new political settlement that renders Britain's EU membership acceptable to the British people and not simply the imposition it is seen as today. Such a political settlement would not simply concern the terms of Britain's EU membership, but also alignment between Britain's strategic concept and an emerging EU concept of strategy. Such an alignment will not prove easy as European integration reflects a very differing strategic culture to that of Britain's. It also too often implies strategic pretence. In September 2014 *The Economist*, commenting on Henry Kissinger's book "World Order" said, "European power, diminished by two world wars, has disappeared down the rabbit-hole of European integration".[95]

Prior to what now seems an almost inevitable in-out British referendum debate the relationship between Brussels and London will remain fractious and uncertain. The challenge as ever is to reconcile British ideas of 'Europe' as an alliance of states, with the federalist ideal of a European super-state. This is nothing new. On 11 May 1953, Prime Minister Sir Winston Churchill rose to his feet in the House of Commons to attack France for its "anti-British" position and said that Britain had done more than anyone to support

---

[95] "Geopolitics: A Bit of a Mess". *The Economist*, 6 September, 2014

what was then the first attempt to create an integrated European force; the European Defence Community (EDC) Treaty. In that same speech Churchill stated famously that "we are with them but not of them", thus ending any chance Britain would join.[96] Scroll on sixty-plus years and that is pretty much the view of the British people today, however many in the London High Establishment would wish that it were not.

David Cameron's January 2013 "Bloomberg Europe Speech" was meant to have marked the start of a sustained effort to deal with the tensions over Britain's place in the EU. He appeared at last to have finally grasped the huge strategic significance of what is happening on the European Continent and had decided to focus on those strategic factors vital to Britain and its national strategy. Indeed, whatever the many challenges facing the EU Britain's European partners still represent an important pool of capability and capacity. However, Cameron's promise to re-negotiate the terms of Britain's EU membership remains as yet unfulfilled.

To properly leverage influence in Europe Britain must remember its history. The British success in World War Two was to establish a political settlement across much of Western Europe that saw parliamentary institutions emerge that were far more in line with the British system of governance than either the American or certainly the Russian. However, in the absence of strategy the British have repeatedly failed to grasp the opportunity to lead Europe, a failure which has led over the years to a political vacuum which first the French, and now the Germans, filled. Today, Germany leads the EU and the manner by which Britain plays an influence role in a Europe that no longer looks to London for leadership, nor shares its strategic culture, will be a profound strategic challenge for London. Indeed, the 2014 Juncker fiasco only served to demonstrate the extent to which German domestic politics shapes Europe far more than British foreign policy.

---

[96] See Lindley-French J. (2008) "A Chronology of European Security and Defence 1945-2007" (Oxford: Oxford University Press) p 43.

Therefore, the dilemma Britain faces is how to re-establish power as the core component of influence in and over Europe, even if Britain is no longer a core member of the EU. This will be particularly important if Britain leaves the EU because whatever happens, Britain must remain at the core of European security and defence. However, only real military power will afford Britain such influence. And, however weak the security effort across the rest of Europe, the British have no alternative but to engage their fellow Europeans in pursuit of Europe's strategic renovation. Much of the EU security and defence edifice is founded on principles of humanitarian interventionism, regionalism and low-intensity conflicts that are now dangerously out-dated. Indeed, it was the hard strategic realities of military power and Europe's lack of it that the 2013 CSDP Summit did nothing to address, which guaranteed its failure and made Europe weaker not stronger, a weakness the Russians are now exploiting.

The essential challenge for the British is that deeper European political integration is not in the British interest, but increasingly inevitable. This is not least because the essential political impulse for deeper political integration is not to better prepare Europeans to face a hyper-competitive world, but to detach Europeans from the very unforgiving realities of that world – Euro-isolationism. The presidency conclusions of the December 2013 EU Summit were illuminating in this regard and reflected a growing impulse in many Eurozone countries to hand areas of deep national sovereignty to a federalist European Commission, more interested in 'state' building than the provision of effective defence.

In the December 2013 Communiqué the European Council called for "...increased synergies between CSDP and Freedom/Security/Justice actors". In other words, the Communiqué reflected a legalistic rather than a strategic approach to defence and military power and the abandonment of national sovereignty over the use of force. This is something that Britain cannot and must never accept. Indeed, for such a system to work there would need to be a country called 'Europe'. Therefore, the battle the British should be fighting over the EU is fundamentally an existential battle yet there are few signs that London understands that. Indeed, the danger for Britain is that as it cuts British forces so it cuts an essential component of what is left of London's power to influence defence policy in Europe, and by extension the centrality of the state in Europe. If that happens NATO over time will also lose the ability to set the standards for defence co-operation and cohesion and the transatlantic strategic relationship will also be gravely weakened.

The European Defence Agency (EDA) is an example of the tension between the inter-governmental idea of Europe and political integration that is weakening Europe. Although it is a relatively small and intergovernmental institution reading between the lines of the December 2013 Communiqué it is evident that the Commission is very keen to rapidly expand the remit of the EDA and eventually make it a 'communitarian', rather than an intergovernmental body. Specifically, the EDA has been charged with "military capability development", designed to build on two legally binding Defence Procurement Directives which were agreed back in 2009.

And yet a new balance between inter-governmental governance and political integration must be found. With nineteen EU member-states spending less that €4bn per annum on defence the appeal of a defence Eurozone with a super-EDA at its core is attractive to many.[97] Critically, such steps would effectively mark the beginning of the end for many EU member-states because without control over defence national sovereignty would become meaningless. In other words, for Britain full sovereign defence integration would be nothing short of a political disaster, even if some elements of defence integration are inevitable especially for smaller EU member-states. Striking the right balance will thus be central to Britain's European diplomacy.

Critically, the British must attempt to re-focus its European partners on strategic power, rather than institution-building. Therefore the challenge for the British is to convince fellow Europeans of the need to re-connect European security to world security and that the nation-state is still the best vehicle to realise such a goal. And,

---

[97] Author's own research.

London must do this at a time when the very idea of coercion has been rejected by many Europeans.

Therefore, for the British big state leadership of an essentially inter-governmental EU must remain the critical organising principle in Europe, built on an EU that supports its member-states, but does not seek to replace them. That will place particular importance on a close set of strategic relations with France and Germany in particular.

Britain and France

The November 2010 Franco-British Defence and Security Co-operation Treaty, together with air operations over Libya in 2011, confirmed the importance of the Franco-British strategic relationship. London and Paris share a classical state-to-state strategic defence relationship that is as important as it is complex. Paris was less than complimentary about the support it received from Britain for their Mali intervention, even though France seems to have conveniently forgotten France's unwillingness to support the British where it mattered in Afghanistan. However, France's decision to suspend the sale of two *Mistral*-class amphibious/command ships to the Russian Navy has been welcomed by London and rightly so.

For all those irritations it is hard to over-state the importance of the Franco-British relationship. Indeed, if the strategic utility of NATO depends to a very great extent on Britain's strategic relationship with the Americans, the future of European defence is still dependent on the Franco-British military relationship, and an increasingly important British-German politico-strategic relationship. A close strategic partnership with France is clearly in the interest of both countries because of the quality and indeed limitations of their respective armed forces. Recent French operations in 2013 have confirmed that. The challenge Paris faced when four thousand French troops arrived in Mali in February 2014 was complicated to say the least. Tuareg tribesmen had taken control of northern Mali and sought separation. They were supported by a particularly nasty bunch of Islamists (Al Qaeda in the Islamic Maghreb and the Mujao)

131

who had profited from the chaos in neighbouring Libya. To make things worse, the Malian Army (or what was left of it) was in meltdown and the country's political system with it.

The success of *Operation Serval* was built on strategic unity of effort and purpose in Paris and underpinned by speed, mass, precision and pressure. This is an approach to operations Paris shares with London. French forces operating alongside unexpectedly effective Chadian colleagues drove back the Tuareg separatists and their Islamist partners. And, the very shock of the French intervention helped open up deep divisions between the two insurgent groups.

The French Air Force proved particularly effective, not least in co-ordinating both logistics and a range of allies and *ad hoc* partners under French command. Critically, France was unequivocally in the lead and for the first time US and allied forces operated to some effect under French operational command. In a sense French success is testament to the years of joint training and efforts to improve interoperability between French and allied forces. Indeed, *Operation Serval* is now a model for the force generation and command of a complex coalition, something that could well become the norm.

French forces were also willing to recognise where and when they needed support, particularly for strategic airlift (from Americans, British and interestingly Russians), air-to-air refuelling and intelligence, surveillance and reconnaissance (the Americans and others).

However, for all the undoubted military success two other factors proved critical. First, the speed of President Hollande's political reaction was vital. Within hours of the Presidential go-decision French aircraft took off from Saint Dizier air base and flew ten hours to strike key targets in Northern Mali. These strikes knocked the Islamist/Separatist coalition off-balance from which they never recovered. These strikes were followed rapidly by the deployment of particularly effective French Special Forces. Like the British in Sierra Leone in 2000, the shock of a front-line Western military force interceding was sufficient to influence events decisively.

Second, the application of political and military tools took place within the framework of deep French historical knowledge of the Malian people, the country and the wider Sahel region. This knowledge was a vital commodity in managing Mali's political and social complexity.

Of vital importance was the strategic 'brand' France represented in the region. Indeed, this was influential because it was not simply 'what' was intervening but 'whom'. This is something Britain's leaders might wish to contemplate as they consider SDSR 2015. Indeed, whilst for the moment Britain's armed forces still have a well-deserved reputation for excellence any more cuts to the forces would certainly damage Britain's strategic brand, possibly critically so.

However, perhaps the most decisive factor in *Operation Serval* was the joined-upness of a French government in crisis. From the President down through the foreign and defence ministries and onto the service chiefs and their force and operational commanders *Serval* was well conceived, soundly-planned and effectively-executed. France was assisted by the strategic and tactical incompetence of their adversaries, as the British were back in the 1982 Falklands War. And, in reality, one rarely gets the chance to choose one's crises. In other words, Mali was 'doable' whereas Afghanistan and Iraq were at the very limits of 'doability'.

It may be that future crises will not be so accommodating to France or her allies. This only serves to reinforce the gap that exists between intervening and succeeding in places such as Afghanistan or the Sahel. Indeed, as the Americans are again finding in their efforts to slow the advance of ISIS in Iraq there is a huge difference between the prevention of genocide (important though that obviously is) and achieving political stability.

Given the dangerous complexity around Europe's southern and eastern borders the lesson for for both Britain and France is clear; they must overcome tactical differences and work together strategically. This means building on the putative Combined Joint Expeditionary Force (CJEF) to bring real European military substance to both NATO 2020 and the EU's Common Security and Defence Policy (CSDP). The need is pressing.

Britain and Germany

The irony of the contemporary European debate is that when all the 'Euro-speak' is stripped away the central question at issue is still in many ways Germany and its power, as it has been since 1871 and the formal unification of Germany at the Palace of Versailles. Today's EU is becoming dangerously close to being an instrument for German leadership, something few in Berlin either seek or desire. Indeed, for all Europe's financial travails one hundred years on from World War One 'Europe' is still to an extent a metaphor for how to accommodate Germany; friend Germany, ally German, partner Germany but nevertheless powerful Germany. Therefore, how Britain relates to Germany will go a long way to establishing Britain's future Euro-strategic trajectory and indeed Europe's world-strategic trajectory. It could also help legitimise Germany's leading role in Europe and thus afford Europeans all-important political balance.

Equally, one cannot separate the strategic from the political in Europe. Two specific challenges will need to be addressed if Britain and Germany are to establish a durable strategic partnership. First, Britain will find it hard to acknowledge German leadership if that leadership is seen to subjugate London to Berlin's will. Second, France would undoubtedly see any accommodation between London and Berlin as a threat to its own 'special relationship' with Germany. To assuage French fears the Franco-British defence-strategic partnership will need to be acknowledged as such by Berlin, with Germany prepared to offer political and practical support to British and French leadership in European security and defence. However, for any such Franco-British-German strategic partnership to thrive, Berlin must accept that Britain will not join the Euro and assist London establish a new and equitable relationship with the true core of EU – the German-led Eurozone.

Nor is the challenge simply one of strategy for there is a profound tension in Europe between state and institutional power that the

134

Eurozone crisis has put into stark relief and which needs to be resolved once and for all. Indeed, although Germany is clearly Europe's leading political power the whole point of the EU is to constrain and not aggregate big power. Consequently, there is a philosophical gulf at the heart of the EU that will also need to be finessed if Britain is to remain a member of the Union and the EU and its member-states are to face rather than duck strategic reality. It will thus fall to Germany to finesse such a new political settlement (for that is what it will take) if that is Germany really wants Britain to remain in the EU.

The essential tension between Britain and much of the rest of the EU is London's concern that the EU is fast becoming a mutual impoverishment pact, unwilling and unable to compete in the twenty-first century world, and that the EU far from promoting a competitive Europe, will actively seek to prevent it by creating a protectionist Europe. Thankfully, Germany and several other leading Western European states, such as the Netherlands and Sweden, also share these concerns. Therefore, it should not be beyond the wit of British and indeed German diplomacy, to establish a joint project to help combat the excessive statism and over-regulation that will sooner or later condemn the EU to failure, and Europeans to poverty.

The test of Germany's *bona fides* vis-à-vis the British and Britain's relevance to a German-focussed EU, will not for the first time in Europe's history involve some issues of military power. Again, this is because the use of force is the first and last preserve of the functioning state. As Anthony King points out, "European forces are now developing transnational relations at ever lower levels which would have been inconceivable during the Cold War. There is no prospect of a European army, however, in which nationality becomes irrelevant as members commit forces to a supranational command structure answering to the EU".[98] However, it is the threat that European integration will in time spill-over into defence that is

---

[98] King, Anthony (2011) "The Transformation of Europe's Armed Forces: From the Rhine to Afghanistan", (Cambridge: Cambridge University Press) p 45.

one of the factors pushing Britain away from the EU, and Germany must help prevent that.

Therefore, it is at the juncture between power and institutions that Britain and Germany must focus European strategy and to that end London and Berlin must understand the importance of Britain's armed forces as a key tool of influence. Indeed, for all the talk of 'Europe' that is bandied around by ever-bolder European federalists the core issues of Europe's place in the world, and Britain's place in Europe still essentially concern state power.

Critically, the British must be in a position to exert active influence on all of its European partners to better invest in security and defence, and such pressure will only be generated if Britain is leading by example. Implementation of the NATO Strategic Concept, NATO 2020 and Smart Defence are the essential components of a revitalised Alliance. The development of the EU's Common Security and Defence Policy (CSDP) could lead to an EU ready and able to fill the political security space in and around Europe, albeit consequent upon NATO's role as a strategic hub based on a new triangular US-NATO-EU security relationship. Britain needs to be at the core of all such developments, and such a goal will only be realised by a Britain committed to a strategic role and the powerful armed forces that would underpin such a role. SDSR 2015 must reflect that ambition.

Britain's World-Wide Strategic Security Web

There is one final lesson to which the British must pay heed if they are to prosper in this globalised age; London's strategic partnerships cannot simply be focused on Europe or the transatlantic relationship. There are other partnerships the British need to foster, all of which will require powerful and credible British armed forces to demonstrate London's strategic ambition and resolve. Indeed, central to British national strategy must be a vision that places partnerships on an equal footing to alliances, via a world-wide security web of democracies. One important lesson for the British from Afghanistan is that it is in the so-called *Anglosphere* where the

British find their most reliable allies; the US, Australia, Canada and, by extension, other Commonwealth countries.

The US, Australia and Canada were the states that were prepared to take significant casualties in Afghanistan alongside the British in Regional Command South and elsewhere. This *Anglosphere* acted in stark contrast to most other Europeans who routinely and determinedly enmeshed themselves in 'national caveats' and cited 'red cards', thus undermining NATO's strategic and operational cohesion. The oft-heard argument from Europeans that the country with the most caveats was the Americans is spurious and self-serving. The Americans did 90% of the fighting and their caveats were designed to preserve the mission not to avoid it. Furthermore, much of the critical and relevant development work being undertaken on Britain's Future Force is taking place not with fellow Europeans, but in informal strategic groupings such as the ABCA (America, Britain, Canada, and Australia). This is a particularly important group for the development of high-end enablers such as future shared strategic intelligence, C4ISR and electronic warfare. If these new/old strategic partnerships are to be properly re-established the concept of British strategy must once again be established on credible power.

In other words, Britain's national political strategy is utterly reliant upon Britain's security and defence strategy because it is the latter 'currency' which generates influence and which thus informs grand alliances. At its core British strategy must thus have powerful, projectable, advanced, deployable armed forces. Therefore, Britain must take the lead in the radical development of radical armed forces armed with sufficient capability and capacity to go wherever problems emerge as they undoubtedly will.

Britain needs flexible forces able and capable to perform a range of roles from high-end combat through stabilisation and onto recovery and reconstruction, which are central to a pioneering whole-of-government concept of deployed power. Indeed, Britain's armed forces will remain the very cornerstone of Britain's foreign and security power and prestige in what is going to be a very bumpy twenty-first century.

Therefore, if Britain's grand alliances, partnerships and the international institutions vital to British strategy are to be made to work for Britain the exercising of British power and the rebuilding of British influence must in turn demand a radical overhaul of British strategy. That goal in turn demands a profound shake-up of the stale, inward-looking and unimaginative British High Establishment so that Britain's political and bureaucratic system of leadership and security governance is again up to the challenges posed. That means the effective exercising of statecraft.

5.

National Strategy: Exercising British Statecraft

"The worst pain a man can suffer: to have insight into much and power over nothing".

Herodotus

The making of strategy is not rocket science. It is politics that makes it seem so. National strategy involves first strategic understanding, the ability, means and capacities to understand the nature of power and change and one's place in that order. Thereafter, such understanding must be applied to the establishment of priorities which in turn become national strategic objectives established themselves on an agile understanding of critical, vital, essential and general interests. Reasoned decisions must then be taken as to the national means to be applied to realise identified ends and the ways by which to do it - statecraft.

Such decisions thus require a balance to be struck between the investments to be made in external engagement and internal security, and between civilian (diplomacy, trade promotion, aid and development) and military and industrial means. Once the means have been identified and invested in then the best way to organise must be considered together with the tools and instruments generated to assess outcomes. Of course, in the real world such strategic judgements (for that is what they are) take place in parallel, but that is the essential challenge of crafting the national strategy essential to the successful conduct of statecraft.

Britain in 2015 needs a powerful instrument at the top of government for the generation, direction and enactment of strategy that itself reflects a whole-of-government approach to international engagement. To that end, the National Security Council must be strengthened and given the necessary prime ministerial authority to fulfil such a role.

The Confusion of Values with Interests

Russia's aggression against Ukraine and the January 2015 Paris attacks were both wake-up calls. In the face of such aggression those responsible for British strategy should thus pose five questions. What are Britain's strategic objectives? How does Britain achieve these objectives? Is there sufficient unity of vision, will and effort to generate such effect? Are there sufficient resources available? What planning traction is needed, where, when and how to achieve objectives? Is there appropriate machinery within and across government to translate strategy into action?

Strategy requires a considered level of ambition backed up by sound organisation and sustained investment. Short-termism kills sound strategy and short-termism is endemic in the way British governments conceive of both strategy and policy. Moreover, the wielding of influence and the pursuit of the national interest are contentious issues in contemporary Britain. Consequently, the debate over Britain's role in the world, given the failure to achieve stable governance either in Iraq or Afghanistan, highlights the essential dilemma London faces about how and where best to use Britain's still not inconsiderable power in the contemporary world. Indeed, if national power is the amalgam of all capabilities and capacities a country can bring to bear through sound strategy, then it must first be conceived and organised at the highest-level of government.

The current focus of government is twofold; fixing Britain's acute financial challenges and maintaining some level of cohesion in a badly-divided strategy. However, there is a danger that the single-minded focus on deficit-reduction, vital though it is, could confirm forever an abandonment of national strategy and thus a future Britain that will punch decidedly below its weight.

To a significant extent contemporary British decline is not so much a reflection of a fundamental shift in power away from Britain, but rather a vacuum in ideas, a lack of will, and the absence of strategic creativity in the London High Establishment. This retreat is reinforced by the loss of direction evident in the defensiveness and muddle over the balance to be struck between Atlanticism and Europeanism, soft and hard power, protection and projection. These divides, and the lack of rigour they reflect in British strategic rigour, were evident throughout both NSS 2010 and SDSR 2010.

Clearly, a propensity for believing Britain permanently-weakened would to some extent be understandable. Britain today is emerging from an unprecedentedly deep strategic and economic slump triggered by a perfect storm as the 2008 banking near-collapse, the Eurozone sovereign debt crisis, and the failure of American strategic leadership, combined to leave Britain shorn of its traditional policy and strategy anchors. Chancellor George Osborne said in his Autumn Statement on 5 December 2013 that the British economy had shrunk by 7.8% between the beginning of the banking crisis in 2008 and the end of 2009.[99] And yet by July 2014 Britain's economy had returned to 2008 levels and was growing at over 3% per annum, faster than any other G7 country.

Therefore, given the nature of emerging challenges, unless the ambition implicit in British strategy recovers in line with the economy (and more), the ability of Britain to influence world events will diminish rapidly. However, closing the all-too-apparent strategy vacuum at the top of government will require a new approach to security and defence that will itself demand much greater unity of effort and purpose across government. Indeed, unless urgent and co-ordinated action is taken to establish innovative strategy that looks beyond the immediate horizon Britain will remain decidedly behind both the threat and influence curves.

To pursue a successful interest-led strategy today London must avoid the open-ended humanitarianism that so defined Britain's world-view during the Blair years. Indeed, open-ended armed humanitarianism has imposed a terrible cost on Britain's armed forces. Equally, there can be no security for Britain at the other extreme of non-engagement, which in the wake of failed campaigns in Afghanistan and Iraq and over Libya, seems to be the prevailing political and popular mood.

---

[99] BBC Daily Politics, "Autumn Statement Special", BBC TV, 5 December 2013.

In a sense, Britain must again learn to be tough enough to be tough and put the greatest effort into those areas most likely to secure Britain's national interests. Indeed, only by re-positing strategic choices on such a sound footing will national strategy have any chance of being cost-effective, successful and by extension help the values of internationalism that are implicit in Britain's foreign engagements.

However, the striking of such a new balance between values and interests will require of Britain's political and bureaucratic elite rigorous, independent analysis of the emerging strategic environment and Britain's national interests. Since at least 1956 British leaders have too often either sought refuge in America's sometimes dangerously one-dimensional strategic prescriptions, or deliberately neutered British influence by embracing a declining Europe (or both), Moreover, Britain has too often succumbed to a form of strategic political correctness, not least in its dealing with former colonial territories.

This intellectual retreat from power has been reinforced by an absence of leadership from the political class which has, in turn, infected the heart of public will to such an extent that not just is Britain's place in the world now open to question, but until the 18 September 2014 referendum on Scottish independence, even the future of the United Kingdom itself (and it would irresponsible to believe the debate over the future of the Union has ended).

Therefore, at the heart of British national strategy must be the political will to re-establish some form and level of British strategic autonomy be it from the Americans, or a self-interested and political Brussels that too often interprets treaty obligations on EU member-states to the maximum and often beyond. Critically, such a reinvigoration of national autonomy would also help reinforce the political union between England, Scotland, Northern Ireland and Wales. However, if such political ambition is to be realised London will need a much more systematic approach to the conceiving, crafting and application of strategy.

Britain's *Little Britain* Dilemma

Britain's politicians too often lurch between seeing Britain as pocket superpower or profoundly impotent. This inconsistency reflects the very political problem Britain has with power. Britain's problem with power and the confusion of values with interests it reflects is further compounded by confusion at the very top of government about the relationship between strategy and management. Sir Lawrence Freedman captures this confusion neatly, "Instead of the deliberate decisions of a few, critics [*of strategy as a concept - author's italic*] pointed to the countless moves of innumerable individuals, unable to see the big picture yet coping as well as they can in the circumstances, leading to outcomes that nobody had intended or desired".[100]

The headless chicken phenomenon is apparent in all of the recent British national security strategies. The stated aim of NSS 2010 was "...to be able to act quickly and effectively to address new and evolving threats to our security". It went on "...that means having access to the best possible advice, and crucially, the right people around the table when decisions are made. It means considering national security issues in the round, recognising that when it comes to national security, foreign and domestic policy are not separate issues, but two halves of one picture".[101] All well and good – but the advice base sought was very narrow and the 'right people' was a typically, and dare one say "Yes Minister", allusion to having only those "around the table" likely to confirm ministerial or high apparatchik prejudice. In other words, British national strategy has become progressively politicised and much of the senior civil service with it.

NSS 2010 was eloquent and erudite but essentially meaningless, a form of strategic PR. Its predecessor, NSS 2008 "...set out how we will address and manage this diverse though interconnected set of

---

[100] Freedman, Sir Lawrence (2013) "Strategy: A History" (Oxford: Oxford University Press) p, xiii
[101] "A Strong Britain in an Age of Uncertainty: The National Security Strategy" (2010) (London: HMSO) p 5.

security challenges and underlying drivers, both immediately and in the longer-term, to safeguard the nation, its citizens, our prosperity and our way of life".[102]

The main concept at the heart of national security strategy should be the interdependence of threats and response and drivers of planning, structure and action that any strategy worthy of its name should generate. Ideally, such an approach would provide for balance between national cohesion, home-base protection, an integrated whole of government response, and the legitimate projection of national power and influence. However, it is hard to see what substantive changes to policy or practice the NSS process (for that is what it has become) has achieved.

Rather, British national security strategies are in keeping with a British security policy tradition that tends to see security and defence as something that government 'does' instinctively. A security policy that tends to emphasise management and short-termism which is reinforced by the absence of dedicated machinery at the heart of government devoted to long-term strategic thinking. This appearance of strategy is typified by a Cabinet Office approach to government which is fast becoming adopted by the National Security Council (NSC) and which actively pursues the confusion of strategy with management – the language of strategy, the ambition of management. In other words, British national strategy is shot through by very British 'muddling through', a weakness that is most evident in how Britain invests in the ways and means to guard against the probable but not very damaging, and effectively ignores the improbable, but potentially highly-devastating.

It is interesting to contrast NSS 2010 with the Japanese National Security Strategy of 17 December 2013. The Japanese strategy is a far more succinct document than its British counterpart and establishes a much closer relationship between analysis of the strategic environment, Japanese interests and the crafting thereafter of considered defence policies and strategies. To that end, the

---

[102] "The National Security Strategy of the United Kingdom: Security in an interdependent world" (2008) (London: HMSO) p 5.

Japanese strategy states, "The Strategy, as fundamental policies pertaining to national security, presents guidelines for policies in areas related to national security, including sea, air, space, cyber-space, official development assistance (ODA) and energy".[103] The challenging geopolitical neighbourhood in which Japan resides clearly focuses the Japanese official mind on the contrast between values and interests far more than the British, and the contrast between the two strategies underlines that dichotomy. This 'focus' was reflected in Prime Minister Shinzo Abe's December 2014 announcement that henceforth Japanese armed forces will be permitted to work with foreign allies and partners beyond the constraints imposed by self-defence.

Whilst the United States is clearly seen as the main recipient of increased Japanese military capability and reach, Britain is also seen by Tokyo as a potentially important partner. This is very much the stuff of grand strategy and harks back to the Anglo-Japanese Alliance of January 1902 when Britain in effect created the Imperial Japanese Navy to help ease the burden on an over-stretched Royal Navy that was facing growing pressure from Imperial Germany in home waters and potentially threats to British imperial lines of communication from Russia. Today, it is the US that is increasingly over-stretched as reductions in defence investment by liberal powers is being matched, and possibly subordinated by, defence investments by illiberal powers, such as China and Russia.

Furthermore, whilst the language used by the Japanese has clearly been influenced by recent British defence reviews unlike Britain Japan confronts its strategic reality head-on: "To ensure peace and security in Japan around the severe security environment surrounding the country, Japan will efficiently develop a highly-effective and joint defence force, adapting to the change in strategic environment with consideration of its national power and the political, economic and social situations; and strive to ensure operations with flexibility and readiness based on joint operations".[104]

---

[103] The National Security Strategy of Japan 17 December 2013. http://kantei.go.jp/foreign/96_abe/documents/2013/_icsFiles/afieldfile/2013/12/17/NSS.pdf p. 2

By contrast NSS 2010 highlights a profound lack of understanding at the top of government in London about the balance to be struck between ends, ways and means. NSS 2010 also highlights a security 'culture of pretence' that has been emerging in Britain for some time by giving the appearance of managing priorities, risks and threats but not in fact doing so. In practice NSS 2010 takes little account of the nature, pace and scope of the grand strategic changes taking place and tends, therefore, to place more importance on affordability than security and defence.

To that end, so-called 'Tier One' threats (important politically and therefore to be planned for) to vital British interests, which are the highest priority for national security, include international terrorism, attacks in cyber-space by other states and large-scale cyber-crime. Only in August 2014 was Russia re-classified a Tier One threat in light of its aggression against Ukraine. Interestingly (and politically) Tier One also includes the danger of a major accident or natural hazards that require a national response, such as flooding or an influenza pandemic. The danger of "an international military crisis between states that could draw in the UK and its allies comes only at the end of Tier One. [105]

Interestingly, an "attack on Britain or its Overseas Territories by another state or proxy using chemical, biological, radiological or nuclear (CBRN) weapons"; risk of major instability, insurgency or civil war overseas which creates an environment that terrorists can exploit to threaten Britain comes only in Tier Two (to be considered rather than planned for). And yet in SDSR 2010 such a threat is identified as the first Military Task. A "significant increase" in organised crime is also deemed a threat to Britain's essential interests, together with severe disruption to information received, transmitted or collected by satellites, possibly as the result of a deliberate attack by another state.

---

[104] Ibidem. P, 15
[105] "A Strong Britain in an Age of Uncertainty: The National Security Strategy" (2010) (London: HMSO) p 27.

Tier Three (talked about, but not really to be planned for) is a kind of catch-all, i.e. threats considered to be of a general nature that are least likely and/or would have the lowest impact. Interestingly, all Tier Three threats pre-suppose strong British control over Britain's borders, which given EU treaty obligations is simply no longer the case. It is only at this level that a large-scale conventional military attack on Britain by another state (not involving the use of CBRN weapons) is considered. Confusingly, such a threat is also bunched together with threats posed by increased terrorism, organised crime, illegal migration and illicit goods trying to cross British borders.

Disruption to oil or gas supplies and/or price instability as a result of war, accident, major political upheaval or deliberate manipulation of supply by producers, a major release of radioactive material from a civil nuclear site within Britain which affects one or more regions is also deemed Tier Three. As is a conventional attack by a state on another NATO or EU member to which Britain would have to respond (Russia in the Baltic States?), or an attack on a British overseas territory as the result of a sovereignty dispute (Falkland Islands) or a wider regional conflict, and short to medium-term disruption to international supplies of resources (e.g. food, minerals, etc.) essential to Britain. Indeed, whilst several, if not all of the above, could very rapidly become Tier One threats they are deemed by the "risk assessment" to be unlikely, and therefore not significant planning drivers.

What is striking about the threat categorisation is the extent to which those areas involving big, long-term security and defence investments over many years are the threats deemed least likely. And yet the figures for defence expenditure by illiberal powers suggests otherwise, as do events on the ground. There are also plain contradictions in the thinking which highlight again the degree to which politics polluted strategy in NSS 2010. For example, nuclear war is deemed highly-unlikely, but nevertheless there is continued significant investment in the nuclear deterrent. In other words, the NSS fails the test of sound strategy-fying because important though the establishment of such priorities undoubtedly are NSS 2010 betrays an essentially partial, political, and often disconnected approach to the 'strategic' choices made thereafter, as though it is more shopping list than strategy. Not only does this again suggest a confusion of values with interests and strategy with management, it yet again betrays politics masquerading as strategy.

Although the word 'global' is mentioned throughout NSS 2010, it is done so only as a function of a determinedly regional focus (with a determined focus on what security can be afforded, rather than what security needs to be afforded). A 'real' national security strategy would highlight the pace and nature of change and call for a much more radical understanding by the British of their strategic environment and its governance, if aforesaid strategic change and transition are to be successfully influenced and managed. Indeed, the comforting illusion that Britain is a status quo power and that Britain automatically benefits from the current international system is one that itself reflects complacency rather than analysis and strategic judgement.

The failure of NSS 2010 is essentially one of ambition. Indeed, whilst the document highlights global trends and challenges, it offers only partial and very political solutions. Indeed, tinkering with the international system works all well and good at times of relative calm, but what NSS 2010 lacks is a big British idea about how Britain might shape or even cope with systemic change. The focus of NSS 2010 is thus very much the here and now and as such fails to address the relationship between Britain's security, British national means, and large strategic ends over time, cost and distance. Rather, like British policy in the 1930s, NSS 2010 trades capability for time in the hope that 'something might come up'. Consequently, NSS 2010 is a political, rather than a strategic document.

Such a confusion of politics with strategy is profoundly dangerous and a quintessential definition of false security. For example, NSS 2010 states at the outset, "We need to understand the context within which we operate in order to protect our security, achieve our national objectives and maintain our influence in world affairs". And yet NSS 2010 patently fails to deliver on that mission in terms of either coherent strategy or policy.[106] Again, before such a mission

---

[106] "A Strong Britain in an Age of Uncertainty: The National Security Strategy"

148

can be fulfilled, national security strategy would need to properly address the relationship between vital, essential and general British interests which it singularly fails to do. An effective national security strategy would also properly enunciate the necessary strategic and policy choices implicit therein. Instead the document effectively implies there is no such relationship between cause, choice and effect, or ends, ways and means.

NSS 2010 also reveals the extent to which *Little Britain* has become part and parcel of *Little Europe*. Indeed, NSS 2010 has much more in common with the EU's 2003 European Security Strategy (ESS) than the US National Security Strategy. That is both good and bad. Good in that NSS 2010 offers a broad sweep of the security environment, emphasising the non-military nature of many challenges; bad in that NSS 2010 reinforces the tension between Britain's European political instinct to civilianise security policy as much as possible and the American tendency to militarise security policy, and thereafter finds no balance between the two.

Critically, NSS 2010 offers no clear set of planning priorities, and planning drivers are at best implicit and mostly wrong. This weakness is reflective of Britain's lack of strategic autonomy over a long period, and a belief that Britain is no longer a major power, even if all the stats demonstrate quite clearly Britain is. In other words, Britain's political and bureaucratic elite simply no longer believe in Britain.

Consequently, NSS 2010 fails to give proper guidance to security planners beyond the most general. Rather, the focus is at the level of declaratory policy, placing much more emphasis on the image of security than the substance of security, and thus too often retreats into essentially meaningless 'apple pie and motherhood' language, such as the need to reinforce multilateral institutions. Ultimately, NSS 2010 is very much a child of comprehensive spending reviews (a government euphemism for cuts), and is thus deliberate in its vagueness, with the main political aim being to prevent government being tied to any particular security commitment beyond the most

(2010) (London: HMSO) p 5.

informal. Consequently, NSS 2010 lacks either imagination or strategic judgement, and is thus more wish-list than strategy.

Worse, NSS 2010 suggests that far from being the first duty of the state security is purely discretionary and thus has a lower policy priority than, say, health, education and/or welfare. The 2013 Comprehensive Planning Review reinforced this bottom-up, 'how much security can we afford' approach to British strategy because it again assessed security simply by the measure of affordability - with the possible and partial exception of cyber-defence - the security fashion of the moment.

This inherent tendency to place the financial cart before the strategic horse is nothing new. Indeed, the very question of what comes first – money or strategy – is, to further mix metaphors, THE chicken and egg question all states must confront. However, successive British governments have chosen austerity in place of strategy, precisely when austerity demands strategy. Britain is slowly emerging from a very real financial and economic crisis to face a very different world from even a decade ago. Sadly, austerity is fast becoming an alibi for declinism and a means of avoiding this dangerous new world. Critically, the NSS process points to but does not fully reveal another essential dilemma; the extent of Britain's interests and the strategy needed to defend them may actually be beyond London's ability to afford it. It is a 'Little Britain' dilemma Britain has faced since at least the 1950s. Does Britain alter its strategy, seek additional resources or seek alternative strategies to safeguard interests? NSS 2010 simply makes no attempt to resolve that dilemma.

Therefore, NSS 2010 is at best an exercise in public relations and at worse an exercise in denial. Indeed, what specific proposals there are in NSS 2010 too often tend to emphasise an unhappy settlement between the main spending departments (welfare, health and education) and those departments of state charged with external engagement (Foreign and Commonwealth Office, Defence and International Development). If a re-elected Cameron government does indeed make the further major cuts to defence it is implying then 2015 will only see that tension grow SDSR 2015 will become another exercise in wilful decline.

In other words, the entire culture of 'national strategy', and the statecraft it implies, has become in Britain a decidedly inside-out, bottom-up approach to security and defence that too often offers little or no basis for proper whole-of-government planning, and thus no reasoned balance between ends, ways and means. Indeed, although NSS 2010 is built around a National Register of Risks that is updated annually, and which was an important innovation, the result is too often a curious mix of partial analysis, unclear intent, political rather than strategic aspiration, and above all, spin.

Therefore, national 'strategy' in Britain fails because it never actually addresses THE pivotal question; what are Britain's strategic goals in the early part of the twenty-first century and what is London going to do to secure them? Steady as you go is fine for a country at the very top of power, but not a particularly good idea for a state that is no longer central to the calculation of allies and partners, and no longer taken seriously by potential adversaries. In other words, the British elite idea of 'strategy' has come to reflect the worst of all strategic worlds and a culture of government that is essentially complacent about the first duty of the state – the security of the citizen.

A Comprehensive Security Approach to the Making of British Strategy

For all its failings the concept of a national security strategy is important. The 1998 Strategic Defence Review (SDR) was a necessary (and ultimately failed) attempt to match the size and shape of the British armed forces to Britain's commitments and assumed interests. However, the methodology implicit in SDR, and by extension the NSS and SDSR processes, if infused with political leadership and proper oversight could work. Ideally, the aim in time should be to create a real whole-of-government approach to national strategy which Britain desperately needs to fashion. However, to realise such a goal, new machinery at the top and in the heart of government will be needed to integrate analysis and prescription in

151

support of long-term strategy, and thereafter its sustained and consistent application across government. Instead, whilst much ink has been spilled championing the much-vaunted integrated approach, too often Whitehall's reality is of Permanent Under-Secretaries (heads of ministries) squabbling over ever-declining budgets.

Consequently, Whitehall has become a 'Potemkin village', which is revealed routinely by even the slightest of shocks. In fact, for a power such as Britain to establish credible strategy, a whole-of-government approach must be the *sine qua non* of future national security. In other words, strategy must drive structure, rather than structure drive strategy. Moreover, British strategy will also require a much closer partnership with an informed public who have been lulled into a sense of false security in spite of (or rather because of) Britain's foreign engagements. For too long successive governments have pretended to the British people that foreign engagements imply little or no impact on their lives, be it higher taxes, reduced welfare or even personal loss. Whilst conceptually the need for a national security strategy is correct, as is the need to generate a big security picture to promote the coherent application of all national instruments that will only happen if the British people see and understand the need.

Nowhere is this 'triumph' of politics over strategy more evident than in Britain's aid and development policy. Indeed, the Overseas Development Act (ODA) has become totemic of the gap between the enunciation of strategy, the generation of British strategic influence, and the method and application of strategy. When the ODA was under the writ of the Foreign and Commonwealth Office Britain's foreign aid was closely co-ordinated with its foreign and security policy. With the creation of the Department for International Development (DfID) that linkage was effectively broken and replaced with vague and general commitments, such as the alleviation of global poverty. And, although a degree of 'conditionality' has recently been restored to promote value for British taxpayer's money, the culture within DfID remains both independent of national strategy and overwhelmingly input-driven. Too much of Britain's aid effort is aid for aid's sake, does little for Britain, and is thus a waste of money.

152

Furthermore, being nice is not in and of itself national strategy. Whilst clearly a British interest, in the broadest sense, reducing global poverty can hardly drive national strategy or policy as the gap between the desired end and the required inputs are too wide for a country the size and wealth of Britain, which itself faces profound social and economic challenges. Indeed, not only does the ODA undermine British strategic effect by diverting resources away from real British interests, but at 0.7% of GDP aid and development actively starves over-stretched British forces and resources elsewhere. In February 2013 David Cameron hinted that British forces could draw on the aid and development budget for peacekeeping operations as part of the so-called Conflict Pool. If that ever happens then it would be a welcome realignment between the use of British taxpayer's money and the British national interest.[107] Sadly, the proposal has become mired in the Whitehall political swamp and the politicised battle between advocates of soft and hard power.

Consequently, Britain faces a profound strategic conceptual problem that, in the absence of a true national strategy, makes it difficult to strike a critical balance between protection of the home base and the projection of power and influence. Furthermore, unless both NSS 2015 and SDSR 2015 truly answer the most pertinent question, how precisely to organise British power, it will be *faux strategie* like all of its successors. At the very least, principles of effective national strategy must be re-established in both NSS 2015 and SDSR 2015. Concepts such as liberal humanitarianism and/or liberal interventionism were all well and good in the 'inter-bellum' between 1989 and 2001 but they look like candy floss wishful thinking in the hard-edge big world Russia is leading Europe towards. Critically, if such political devices become confused with vital national strategic

---

[107] According to The Times six of the eight countries receiving the largest aid from Britain totalling £1.5bn have or are about to launch space programmes. See "Critics ask why Britian is giving £1.5bn in aid to countries with space ambitions" "The Independent", 10 August, 2013. http://www.independent.co.uk/news/uk/politics/critics-ask-why-britain-is-giving-15bn-in-aid-to-countries-with-space-ambitions_8755751.html

interests they could all too easily lead Britain down a dangerous road that would prevent the making of hard but sound strategic choices.

Furthermore, it is neither Britain's place nor Britain's role to make the world a happy place. Human suffering is such that it is beyond the scope of the British to resolve, whatever the pressures brought to bear on politicians by the BBC, Sky and their ilk. Rather, British influence must re-focus on preparing for the actions most likely to secure and defend Britain's vital and essential interests given the resources, culture, capabilities and capacities that Britain and its people can bring to bear. Given the nature of Britain a by-product of such focus would undoubtedly be a safer and thus happier world. At the very least London needs to understand that it is precisely the defence of British interests that will most likely promote British values. Any alternative is not strategy, but simply gesture.

The Critical National Security Council

So, can Britain establish a new strategic culture essential to the conduct of sound statecraft? To do so Britain would need appropriate machinery to formulate, review and implement national strategy. That must involve senior ministers, certainly the Prime Minister and the Chancellor of the Exchequer, as well as the Secretaries of State for Foreign Affairs and Defence. Those ministers need in turn to receive appropriate advice formulated by officials putting forward coherent choices reflecting assessed strategic issues, both short and long-term. This does not happen in practice, partly because ministers are unwilling to engage in this way, and partly because the machinery to formulate coherent strategic advice does not exist. In the British system the pulling together of departmental interests and indeed cross-government policy, should be the task of the Cabinet Office, Cabinet committees and the Cabinet itself. However, the Cabinet is too large, has too many concerns, and does not devote sufficient time to matters of strategy.

An attempt to remedy this profound failing was made with the creation of the National Security Council (NSC) on 12 May 2010. The NSC is a mixed ministerial and official Cabinet committee

154

chaired by the Prime Minister. However, in spite of the similarity of name, the British NSC does not, nor can have, the authority of its American counterpart. Indeed, the British NSC could work as an effective strategy body only if ministers are prepared to consider in the round longer-term issues they have not been nor show signs of being willing so to do. In other words, whilst the setting up of the NSC may have been marginally helpful in promoting consistency across government until it derives authority from ministers in a manner, and to an extent, necessary to overcome departmental divisions, the absence of an appropriate strategic culture will continue and with it a failure to match issues with resources. The strategic vacuum at the top of British government and national strategy will thus continue.

What Britain really needs is a politically-heavyweight National Security Council. The need for a comprehensive security approach, tight strategy, and its application across government is vital. Therefore, the National Security Council should be central to Britain's national security transformation and given the necessary weight within government to force synergy on reluctant departments of state. To that end, the NSC should be overseen by a Cabinet-level Security Minister with sufficient authority and stature to drive the competing bureaucracies towards defined national strategic objectives. Realistically, the development of such a figure within government would take many years because to be effective a security minister would need status similar to that of today's Chancellor of the Exchequer, i.e. second only to the Prime Minister. However, if policy, strategy and structure are to become much tighter the NSC MUST be led by just such a political heavyweight.

Furthermore, for the NSC to carry the necessary authority within government the Prime Minister's heavyweight engagement, as necessary directing and controlling the three principal departments (as well as the Treasury), would also be required. This has not happened and does not appear at all likely. The result is that there is no national strategy, and no coherent set of national sub-strategies, to resolve tensions between desired policies and resource constraints. Consequently, the essential transmission of policy into strategy fails and it is for this reason why British strategy so often falls prey to politics.

Therefore, in spite of appearances and protestations to the contrary, Britain lacks an effective mechanism for the scanning of strategic horizons, the crafting of consequent objectives, and the making and fulfilment of appropriate strategy. Soldiers talk these days of the 'strategic corporal', a relatively low-level actor the actions of whom have strategic implications. The same could be said, albeit with perhaps more eloquence, for diplomats and diplomacy. Tactics necessarily operationalise strategy at the lower levels of effect and, as such, are central to the organisation of effort, resources and human capital. This is particularly the case when 'priorities' emerge from a bewildering array of values and interests – the value-interest.[108] This dilemma is made even more acute when ministers also regularly confuse the tactical with the strategic given their need to service the voracious twenty-four hour news cycle.

British Statecraft

The exercising of British strategy will also be dependent on the British re-learning the arts (occasionally dark arts) of statecraft, and the skilful management of international relations which they once pioneered. Such statecraft has been steadily abandoned over the past fifty or sixty years of decline. This abandonment has proved disastrous for Britain which is unusually dependent on the successful generation, leading and shaping of a range of strategic partnerships, some for specific crises, and others of a more enduring nature. Indeed, statecraft demands in turn the skilful exploitation of all national means, supported by sound strategic judgement in the crafting and maintenance of alliances and partnerships, and through the extensive use of effective international institutions and regimes. Above all, exercising strategy requires of the British the means of influence (power), the organisation of influence (structure), and the

---

[108] Henry Kissinger warned against the implied self-imposed paralysis of value-interests. "…no country has the capacity to impose all its preferences of the rest of mankind, priorities must be established". Kissinger, Henry (2004), "Diplomacy" (New York: Touchstone) p 814.

currency of influence (prestige). To that end, British strategy SHOULD be founded on Britain's abiding and defining ability to organise and leverage others in pursuit of national security policy goals. Today, as Britain's absence during the February 2013 Minsk cease-fire talks on Ukraine attests, that is no longer the case.

Therefore, given the nature, extent and scope of strategic change, and the relative and still significant military, economic and cultural power that given the will Britain could still muster, with the correct judgements London could continue to shape change to a significant extent. However, such a strategic aim must also be reflected in the national level of ambition that drives British statecraft. Indeed, given the nature of the contemporary global order (and disorder) the British will not find security through any form of bureaucratic pacifism, as seems to be the creed across much of Continental Europe, and which has been so starkly revealed by Russia's 2014 aggression in Eastern Europe. Statecraft thus means Britain's leaders armed with strategic options and the necessary influence over as many partners and capabilities as possible. That in turn means the power to influence and the skills to exploit it – statecraft.

Nowhere is the effective application of British statecraft more important than in the Special Relationship with the United States. Indeed, the central aim of British statecraft must remain the generation of sufficient power in Washington to influence American policy. Equally, notwithstanding the close defence and intelligence relationship between Britain and the US, British 'influence' will be best served by a degree of autonomy from the Americans. Such autonomy will be essential if British strategic influence is to be realised in Europe and elsewhere, and if British (rather than American) interests are to be served. Paradoxically, such autonomy could lead in time to a more effective and balanced relationship with the Americans, and eventually more influence in Berlin (Europe's critical capital), as the British re-engineer freedom of manoeuvre. Indeed, some level of strategic autonomy would help re-establish Britain's reputation as a creative, honest and free-thinking partner and that in and of itself would help to safeguard and promote British interests.

Although Washington will never permit (and rightly so) Britain a *droit de regard* over US policy the British should nevertheless still aspire to influence the Americans. And whilst the French and Germans will never readily accord Britain an equal voice in the EU, nevertheless Britain should aim to exercise influence over Europeans and the EU reflective of Britain's significant economic, and in European terms, leading military capability. Sadly, too many allies and partners see Britain as either an adjunct to US strategy and/or marginal to Europe. Certainly, British influence in and over Europe has not been at all apparent of late even though what happens on the Continent remains a critical national interest.

Therefore, the British must at one and the same time seek to generate more informal strategic partnerships, whilst at the same time rendering formal partnership more effective, not least via NATO and the EU. The West in the twenty-first century is not a place, but an idea open to all who share its goals and objectives – liberal democracy, free market economics, rule of just law, and human rights. And, whilst echoes of Britain's Greece to America's Rome must continue to resonate in British strategy, renewed British influence could necessarily be generated by a new strategic consensus within a wider West that Britain could help engineer. In other words, Britain must seek to move the strategic goalposts of the West away from what is looking ever more like a Berlin-Brussels-Washington axis that by-passes London.

British statecraft will also require more than a simple re-orientation of strategy. It will also require new strategy not least if London is to close the growing transatlantic security gap that is exaggerating Britain's decline. For many European states following American strategic leadership is now beyond them militarily. And yet (and paradoxically) their very weakness increases their defence dependence on the US, even as it undermines their value as allies to the US. It will fall to Britain to help bridge a gap that is undermining the strategic and political utility of the West. Sadly, far from filling that gap Britain seems to be falling into it. [109]

---

[109] In a 2006 article on NATO the author described the Capability-Capacity Crunch as "an Alliance in which only the Americans can afford both military

Effective statecraft also demands that Britain invest both political and real capital in the tools needed to shape the international environment. Certainly, Britain must urgently look beyond Iraq and Afghanistan and not use both campaigns as excuses for political inaction. [110] Future military interventions will be required and British strategy must thus focus on how best to intervene successfully at the least possible cost in lives, money and politics at a time when peer competitors are emerging and extremism is gathering momentum. Such a focus will in turn place a premium on effective 'upstream' conflict prevention, and both conventional and nuclear deterrence, all of which are to some extent or another dependent on credible strategic and military power.

Furthermore, given the dependence of British national strategy on allies and partners if the British are to restore influence London must also grasp the depth of the crisis in strategy in Britain's allies and partners in the wake of the Afghanistan and Iraq imbroglios. In Europe it is a crisis that has been generated by a determined refusal to look at the big security picture for fear of the strategic and cost implications. The strategic denial from which much of Europe suffers is ironically (and partly) because the very consideration of strategy in Europe causes divisions, particularly within the EU.

The European strategy crisis is particularly apparent in defence as paradoxically the rising cost of military equipment (military capability) critically undermines military capacity at a time when so much public money is being diverted to prop up the Eurozone.

---

capability and capacity most NATO Europeans face a capability-capacity crunch, forced to make a choice between small, lethal and expensive professional military forces or larger, cheaper more ponderous stabilisation and reconstruction forces". See Lindley-French J. (2006) "The Capability-Capacity Crunch: NATO New Capabilities for Intervention" in "Europeans Security", Volume 15, Number 3, 2006 (London: Routledge) pp 259-280

[110] Former NATO Deputy Supreme Allied Commander Lt. General Sir Richard Shirreff said on 12 August 2014, "We have politicians who want to posture, who make a lot of noise but do not have any stick...The government is terrified of any form of intervention involving boots on the ground before an election next year". See, "UK Politicians 'Terrified' of Military Intervention in Iraq – ex-general". Reuters, 12 August, 2014 www.uk.reuters.com/article/2014/08/12/uk-iraq-security-britain-idUKKBN0GC0PK20140812

Consequently, whilst no challenger will likely confront Western forces directly (for the time-being), adversaries and enemies understand that forcing the West to use small but advanced militaries on stabilisation and reconstruction missions rapidly degrades such forces and thus drains them of utility. Even the fear of just how hollowed out European forces have become helps to undermine national, and by extension, European political will.

Worse, the core assumption of British defence strategy that the United States can be relied to be always present in strength is now questionable. The domestic American political and financial situation is forcing Washington to become highly selective about where, when and with whom it wants to act. Moreover, many in the Washington elite either see Britain as an extension of American foreign and security policy, yet another EU member-state, no longer important or a combination of all three. Therefore, British statecraft implies the need for a far clearer, firmer set of self-generated criteria for intervention that takes account not only of the need to maintain important alliances, but also likely long-term consequences for British interests. This is especially the case if the Americans demonstrate the same kind of indifference to the price Britain paid to support the US in Afghanistan and Iraq as shown by the Obama administration. Certainly, London must avoid being sucked into American missions only to see the US move onto other challenges, or forced to act in support of the US when American and British interests do not align.

As President Obama discovered in 2013 when his proposed punitive strike against the Assad regime in Syria was thwarted, US relative decline is also lifting the political threshold for American intervention. This is a perception that has been strengthened not weakened by limited US air strikes against ISIS in northern Iraq. That said, the British (of all America's allies and partners) are in a unique position to influence American security policy and thus reinforce all-important American strategic leadership. However, to do so the British must possess the credible military power to influence Washington, and have the demonstrable will to use such power. Sadly, given Washington's perception of British failure in both Iraq and Afghanistan, London's influence in the US has been sorely weakened. It is decline that was further exacerbated by the American perception that SDSR 2010 was an exercise in wilful decline, which weakened the central pillar of the Special Relationship and, by extension, the transatlantic relationship upon which British strategy has for so long been established.

Therefore, the British will have to consciously strive to restore London's influence in Washington. Such influence will require, first and foremost, statecraft built on a political commitment to reinvest in rebuilt British armed forces. And, whilst the very real limits of British influence in Washington must be firmly understood and thus central to statecraft, in the absence of a strategic Germany or a unified Europe, it will still fall mainly to the British to tie the Americans into European security by demonstrating a willingness to share burdens equitably when US and British interests align.

Lose the Americans and British strategy will become indistinct from that of other Europeans, and in time NATO will fail. Indeed, the Atlantic Alliance is still established on a strong Anglo-American strategic relationship. Furthermore, the British should be pressing on the Americans the value of security community and the idea of a world-wide web of secure democracies. Britain's links with other traditional partners such as Australia and Canada, and possibly India and Japan, would be reinforced by such a concept and with it Britain's importance to Washington. However, if London ducks the statecraft challenge described above given the nature of dangerous change taking place in the world (and in American strategy) the Special Relationship will continue to fade and with it the value and effectiveness of British statecraft.

6.

Defence Strategy: Britain's Radical Future Force

"One clear lesson since the last Strategic Defence Review in 1998 is the need more frequently to reassess capabilities against a changing strategic environment".[111]

If Britain's armed forces are to meet the strategic challenges laid out in this book SDSR 2015 must radically re-think the role, utility and structure of Britain's armed forces if they are to act as the *sine qua non* enabler of British national strategy. That means the realisation of a British Future Force that can operate across and within the seven domains of twenty-first century conflict; air, sea, land, cyber, space, information and knowledge. It must be a core or hub force centred-on the high-end of the conflict spectrum and powerful enough to act at the centre of coalitions comprised of allies and partners alike. Therefore, implicit in Britain's defence-strategy is perhaps the most important strategic question of all; what role does Britain seek to play in the world?

To re-state, SDSR 2010 established seven Military Tasks all of which must be set against "...a changing strategic environment": defending the UK and its overseas territories; providing strategic intelligence; providing nuclear deterrence; supporting civil emergency organisations in times of crisis; defending UK interests by projecting power strategically through expeditionary interventions; providing a defence contribution to UK influence; and providing security for stabilisation.

From Spearhead to Strategy

Speaking at the Royal United Services Institute on 18 December 2013, Chief of the Defence Staff, General Sir Nick Houghton said, "...the current defence paradigm which informs the funding, structure and employment of defence and the armed forces will need

---

[111] "Securing Britain in an age of Uncertainty: The Strategic Defence and Security Review 2010", October 2010 (London: HMSO) p.9.

to evolve in order to meet the emerging defence and security challenges of the age. We are in a situation which thoughtful people should pay attention to, and that the Ministry of Defence, and government more widely, will need to respond to in the years ahead".[112] Houghton's speech highlighted both the good and bad of British strategy, and those charged with it. Good, in that Houghton links the challenges faced by Britain and its armed forces to Britain's strategic environment. Bad, in that the solutions offered go nowhere near far enough, or quickly enough, to fulfil the Military Tasks as specified, given the nature and scope of change in the strategic environment.

The British armed forces are the cornerstone of British strategy and influence, but only as long as they have sufficient levels of high-end military capability, necessary enablers and vital support. In the run-up to SDSR 2015 the Ministry of Defence has instigated what it calls, "Transforming Defence", with the stated aim of delivering "...battle-winning armed forces, a smaller, more professional MoD, and a hard-headed approach to what we can afford".[113] However, given the almost complete shut-down by the Government of any meaningful public debate about Britain's future defence (and the collapse in morale within the MoD), it is hard to discern any political commitment that would commit SDSR 2015 to a well-conceived and balanced assessment of the strategic environment, proper consideration of the future operating environment, the role of Britain therein, and the investment required to make such a Future Force credible. Therefore, if Britain's armed forces are to play their proper role in closing the yawning gap between what Britain needs to do in today's world, and what government seems willing to afford, Britain's armed forces will need a radical re-think.

Strategic ambition is central to effective defence strategy for Britain. *Exercise Joint Warrior* is Europe's and possibly the world's biggest maritime amphibious military exercise. Led by Britain's Royal

---

[112] "Lecture by General Sir Nick Houghton GCB, CBE, ADC Gen, Chief of the Defence Staff, UK Ministry of Defence", Royal United Services Institute, London, December 18, 2013 http://www.rusi.org/events/past/ref:E5284A3D06EFED
[113] "Ministry of Defence Top Level Messages – December 2013".

Navy and 3 Commando Brigade the exercise involves some forty ships from fifteen nations with over forty thousand personnel as part of a Response Force Task Group (RFTG) to enable 'theatre entry' from the sea. This is Britain's global reach maritime-amphibious spear-tip, soon to be strengthened immeasurably with the commissioning of two 65.000 ton aircraft carriers, *HMS Queen Elizabeth* and *HMS Prince of Wales.*

This 'Future Force' if realised (a big if) would afford London reach, flexibility and political discretion during crises, and whilst nothing like as powerful as an American carrier-task group, would be an impressive exercise in power-projection by a single European nation-state. It is precisely the type of force that will be central to the restoration of Britain's strategic influence as it suggests a country that is prepared not just to talk the talk of strategy, but walk the walk.

However, strategic ambition is also the essential problem for London. In theory at least the political utility of such a force is that it offers London a modest, but critical alternative to the Americans as a coalition force generator and leader of choice and thus 'buys' London influence in capitals and institutions far beyond the simply military domain. However, in the absence of sound strategy, London's ability to use its armed forces to influence key allies and institutions is limited, and too often such exercises look like a desperate attempt by Britain's military leaders to convince politicians why the Armed Forces actually exist. Indeed, this author was acutely aware that the only politicians present on Exercise Joint Warrior were Dutch, not British. This is important because one senior Dutch officer admitted to this author that neither the Royal Netherlands Navy nor the Royal Netherlands Marine Corps would likely exist but for their British counterparts, and capable allies are central to British defence strategy.[114]

There is some good news for Britain's armed forces to build upon. Whilst many of Europe's defence budgets are in meltdown Britain has a confirmed defence equipment programme of £160bn over ten

---

[114] Conversation with the author on Exercise Joint Warrior.

years.[115] Take the Royal Navy for example. With the construction of two new super-carriers, the commissioning of Type-45 super-destroyers, the new Astute class nuclear hunter-killer submarines, and with Type-26 frigates and other command and helicopter ships planned (together with the commissioning of the design phase for the four Trident successor ballistic nuclear-missile submarines), over the medium–term Britain could well leave most of its European allies behind in certain vital capability areas (which will generate other challenges). However, all of this investment depends on successive British governments remaining consistent and fulfilling such commitments and the mood music coming from the leaderships of both Conservative and Labour parties suggests the defence budget could again be raided to meet other commitments.

Indeed, SDSR 2015 will fail the ambition implicit in *Joint Warrior* unless London follows through and properly balances ambition, resources and commitments. To that end, the defence review must look upward and outward at the world, and down and deeply into the services because for all the capability developments there are dangerous gaps in Britain's armed forces that will critically limit the effectiveness of the force and increase reliance on often incapable allies. The most notably and dangerous lacuna is in electronic eyes and ears critical for protection of the nuclear deterrent. For example, in December 2014 two Russian hunter-killer submarines attempted to harass one of Britain's ballistic missile submarines. [116] There is little point in investing in strategic assets if they cannot be properly defended and supported.

---

[115] Confirmed in a speech to the RUSI Air Power Conference by the Rt Hon. Philip Hammond MP, London, and 25 October, 2012.

[116] The author was present at RAF Kinloss in late 2010 the proposed home of Nimrod MRA4 the day it was announced that the plane was to be scrapped. It offered Britain autonomous intelligence-gathering and protection capabilities for five of the six main defence roles and was critical to the protection of the submarine-based nuclear deterrent. It would have also been critical to the protection of new aircraft carriers and the Response Force Task Group and was more capable that the American equivalent the P8 that only entered service in 2013. Five had already been built at the time of scrapping and were dismantled.

Organic Jointness: Time for Defence Radicalism

At the core of Britain's defence strategy must be a joint force that is so closely co-ordinated that it represents a true revolution in military affairs – organic jointness.[117] In his RUSI speech Houghton stated, "As far as the force structure is concerned, we must exploit the advent of the Joint Forces Command to champion the enablement of the force. This command is now the proponent for C4ISR, for Cyber, for Special Forces, for Joint Logistics and Defence Medical Services. It owns those things that represent the nervous system of capability. And it has come of age".[118] In fact, the Joint Force Command (JFC) must become far more than a mere proponent. It must drive change and become the defence equivalent of the reformed National Security Council discussed above, and at the very core of robust national strategy.

In other words, it is time for Britain to be defence radical. It was Britain that created the first all-professional force back in 1959. Britain must now create the first truly strategic and organically-generated joint force able to reach back into society to draw upon the widest possible range of skills and talents. The Joint Force Command is a start but it goes nowhere near far enough and, at the very least must have high-level representation from all three services if the Joint Expeditionary Force (JEF) and the Permanent Joint Headquarters at its heart is to be realised as a strategic, rather than an economy force. To that end, a showcase is needed that demonstrates the capacity of British forces to reach and strike and at the same time afford Britain effective command and control of coalitions. In that context jointness mean mean synthesis of all three services into a single-mind-set strategic culture through integrated forces, including where appropriate civilian elements.

---

[117] The book refers to "jointness" rather than the more normal 'jointery' because the aim is to approach a new concept of joint military thought and action.
[118] "Lecture by General Sir Nicholas Houghton GCB, CBE, ADC Gen, Chief of the Defence Staff, UK Ministry of Defence", RUSI 18 December 2013. http://www.rusi.org/events/past/ref:E5284A3D06EFFD

Indeed, it is precisely in the domain of joint and integrated capability that organic jointness is vitally needed. For too long Service chiefs have seen such enabling capabilities as secondary to their own core Service capabilities. That must end. Joint and integrated capabilities are the bedrock upon which the Joint Force must be established and central to the working up of organic jointness. This is vital for effective command and control, strategic situational awareness, and the exploitative, agile mind-set that must support such a command culture. Therefore, JFC must at the very least be given the status and authority to drive organic jointness across the three Services. It should also be given a further role (with supporting capabilities and resources) to reach out to and command if necessary all civilian national means during a national emergency.

To achieve such a radical shift SDSR 2015 would need to mark a clean break from SDSR 2010. SDSR 2010 was what one senior figure called a "spread-sheet review", where balancing the books came well before establishing a coherent strategic military capability.[119] To be fair, this was not surprising given the government back then was faced with unfunded spending commitments of £74bn when it came to power. Former Defence Secretary Philip Hammond was right to suggest that one of his main tasks was to end what he called a "conspiracy of optimism" at the Ministry of Defence and defence equipment. However, balancing strategy with commitments has proven harder than expected and the current conspiracy of declinism is at least as dangerous as any conspiracy of optimism.

Indeed, whilst those who drafted SDSR 2010 understood this requirement and accepted capability "holidays" there was apparently very little linkage between the SDSR's cost-cutting mission and the 'strategy' trumpeted by government – hence strategic shrinkage. SDSR 2010 singularly failed to align resources and commitments, and consequently SDSR 2010's flagship Future Force 2020 (FF2020) is a messy compromise driven more by budget considerations than strategic calculation.[120] The current buzzwords

---

[119] In conversation with the author.
[120] SDSR 2015 states, "...we are delivering this commitment in the context of

168

of MoD-speak – agile, flexible and adaptable – must thus be seen as metaphors for cuts, rather than a strategic concept of jointness or interoperability. At the very least SDSR 2015 must move to resolve these tensions.

The sheer scale and pace of defence cuts has also had a disastrous effect on British influence. SDSR 2010 nominally cut the defence budget by 8% but in reality went far further. Moreover, the June 2013 Comprehensive Spending Review (CSR) 'shaved' a further 7% off what was meant to have been the absolute defence bottom-line. This sent a very negative set of signals to allies, partners and the armed forces themselves, and encouraged those who would welcome diminished British, and by extension Western, influence in the world. Worse, Chancellor George Osborne has indicated that should the Conservative Party win the May 2015 general elections further deep cuts will be made to the public purse with defence again in the line of fire. The consequence of such a further defence cut would be quite simply disastrous for British strategy.

The CSR retained the defence resource budget at £24bn ($37bn) whilst the annual defence equipment budget was fixed at £14bn ($21bn) with a planned year-on-year real-terms increase of 1% up to 2020. However, defence cost inflation is running markedly higher than the allowances incorporated into planning the defence budget, which is still declining in real terms. The Special Military Reserve was cut by £900m in line with the reduction in operational costs with following the withdrawal of British forces from Afghanistan. And, whilst there are no further planned cuts to the numbers of soldiers, sailors and airmen, major cuts are still earmarked for defence civilians and in the officer corps. This will mean either the engagement of expensive contractors, the diversion of military personnel to undertake jobs hitherto done by civilians or simply a reduction of capacity to undertake work. [121] There is of course one

---

inherited defence spending plans that are completely unaffordable. There was an unfunded liability of around £38bn over the next ten years. That is more than the entire Defence Budget for one year". "Securing Britain in an Age of Uncertainty: The Strategic Security and Defence Review", October 2010, (London: HMSO) p 15.

[121] See "Spending Review 2013 – the key points",

other option; cut the nuclear deterrent to fund the conventional force because unless something shifts and the deterrent is again seen as a national (as opposed to purely defence asset) that is probably the only way to balance ends, ways and means.

There are three other lessons critical to the creation of a British strategic force that London must heed. First, quality personnel must be retained. Sadly, too many British personnel with many years of service are seeking to leave or being forced to leave the Armed Forces because changing tax and pension rules effectively make it impossible for them to stay beyond the age of forty.

Second, the force must drive towards much deeper unity of effort and purpose between and across the Royal Navy, Army and Royal Air Force. For example, the Royal Navy's so-called 'harmony' rule is that personnel must be on duty 220 days deployed per annum, the Army's 166 and the RAF 140.[122] On the face of it, this apparent imbalance undermines the ability of Britain's armed forces to deliver the same with less through deeper synergies because it complicates the effective use of the force through efficient force rotation. Indeed, such rules seem to reflect past practice and past deployment patterns, and given changes to force structure, defence roles and tasks (Afghanistan, Iraq, Libya et al) there is a pressing need to review these arrangements.

Third, the endemic tribalism at the higher levels of all three Services must end. Tribalism has done and is doing real damage to the case for national investment in the armed forces. Britain's military leaders will need to radically re-think the way they do business across the security and defence piece. Specifically, Britain's military leaders must demonstrate to both their political masters and the taxpayer they understand the need to develop a single coherent vision. That must mean radical solutions with organic jointness as much about selling the Future Force as fighting and funding it. Above all they must speak with one voice to HM Treasury and use

---

http://www.theguardian.com/politics/2013/jun/26/spending-review-2013-the-key-points The Guardian, 26 June, 2013.
[122] Research carried out by the author during Exercise Joint Warrior, April 2013

SDSR 2015 to such an end. The creation of the Defence Board has gone some way to easing such frictions, but more needs to be done to stop SDSR 2015 descending into yet another inter-Service bidding war.

Semper Fidelis?

Critically, Britain needs a strategic force able to generate credible, sustainable, front-line capability critical to Britain's wider strategic influence. The force must be reinforced by deeper integration between the three services and deeper co-operation across Whitehall and beyond. The vision of an agile, flexible and adaptable force implicit in Future Force 2020 is only a very small first step. A strategically-credible and relevant future force will require of the British a new approach to force and functional interoperability with the British armed forces a hub for inter-force and inter-modal collaboration.

In his speech to the Royal United Services Institute General Houghton bluntly stated the problem; "...we remain too platform-focused and insufficiently concerned about enablers [*such as Maritime Patrol Aircraft* – *author*]. The historic service-centric, major equipment focus has left us with relatively strong environmental components, but devoid of senses and a central nervous system...We are critically-deficient in the capabilities which enable the joint force, such things as intelligence, surveillance, compatible communications, joint logistics and tactical transport".[123]

In the past Britain had three strategic services with which to generate influence almost autonomously from each other. However, in future Britain will have to forge one strategic service, often at high readiness and configured for rapid action in a future operating environment which none of Britain's armed services will 'own' - land, sea, air, space, cyber, information and knowledge, and which all must own. Military innovation will thus be vital, together with a

---

[123] "Lecture by General Sir Nicholas Houghton GCB, CBE, ADC Gen, Chief of the Defence Staff, UK Ministry of Defence", RUSI 18 December 2013. http://www.rusi.org/events/past/ref:E5284A3D06EFFD

'one-ness' mind-set central to organic jointness. That in turn will demand a new and radical balance between force, structure and strategy, and a wholly different use of people.

In effect, the British armed forces must become much more like the US Marine Corps (USMC). The US Marine Corps has everything the British armed forces need and could act as a model for the radical reform needed if London is to balance strategy, capability, capacity and affordability. First, the USMC is organically 'joint' i.e. air, land and sea power automatically work together towards mission success. There is no inter-service rivalry as they are all Marines. Second, organic jointness requires a conscious effort to drive the tri-service culture still apparent into a real force singularity, and the USMC offers just such a model. Third, the USMC is inherently expeditionary with all sea, air and land assets organised in support of expeditionary operations. Fourth, all future, major British operations will be in some form expeditionary with command devolved and airmen, sailors and soldiers rotating through the Joint Force Command. Fifth, the USMC sits at the margins between land operations and maritime/amphibious operations, and it is exactly the strategic 'ground' the British Future Force will be required to occupy for much of its effort.

Organic jointness will also demand and require reform of both the military mind and body. The stated aim of SDSR 2010 was to set Britain on course to a sustainable defence future with the objective a flexible and adaptable Future Force 2020. Frankly, it is more likely to be 2025, even 2030, before the limited defence-strategic vision implicit in SDSR 2010 (and by extension SDSR 2015) is realised.

Whilst much effort must be invested in deepening jointness to create a strategic-operational hub London still insists that the Royal Navy, Army and Royal Air Force should not lose their unique identities which are of themselves strategic brands capable of projecting influence. This is understandable. However, the preservation of identity must not be used by the Services to prevent or slow down the move towards organic jointness. This is because the Future Force must be a thinking force that trains and thinks jointly together, with much greater emphasis placed on experimentation, knowledge and understanding in exercising so that capability can be developed over time via a more scientific application of the military art. Yes, the basic skills of soldiers, sailors and airmen must be honed, but the joint force concept must also hone a joint force mind-set at every level of command.

Such a change in the British military mind-set will not come without friction. Tradition has an important role to play in military art and all too often it blocks military science. Therefore, the process must be driven ruthlessly from the top with changes made to structure, organisation and application if the British are to retain armed forces of sufficient size and scope, and with sufficient quantities of quality equipment across the whole Force, as well as attract and retain the quality people upon which such a necessarily thinking force must be built. This is not just the responsibility of the Defence Chiefs, but more importantly, the Prime Minister, Secretary of State for Defence, the National Security Council, AND the Parliamentary Defence Select Committee.

Measuring Cost against Strategic Value

Many of the problems British forces face are purely political and reflect the triumph of short-term politics over considered strategy and by extension an inability of London to measure cost against strategic value. For example, the decision of the previous Labour government to equip the two new super-carriers with the short take-off and vertical lift (STOVL) version of the F-35 Lightning II was reversed by the Coalition government. However, the cost of installing 'cats and traps' in the carriers became too great and resulted in a June 2012 reversal of that decision, and a subsequent reversion to the STOVL/F-35B version of the F-35. The reason for this reversal was not only to enable the government to bring the defence budget back into balance, but to enable savings so that the second of the two carriers, *HMS Prince of Wales,* could be commissioned into the fleet. Political flip-flopping of this kind does terrible damage to force planning and indeed adds huge cost.

HMS Queen Elizabeth will join the fleet in 2018. The objective is to have a continuously-at-sea force by 2020, that could be 'surged' in an emergency to a two carrier force, with the carriers also acting in both a carrier-strike and littoral manoeuvre capacity able to launch and support land forces from the sea. However, the evolution in the role of the new carriers from carrier-strike to littoral manoeuvre (what is called in the jargon Carrier-enabled Power Projection or CEPP) again highlights the essential tension in British defence strategy, between the short and long-term and again the inability of successive British governments to properly consider cost against strategic value.

The only way to properly address such an essentially political failing is to establish a thoroughly strategic force concept and stick to it. All three Services have prepared vision documents to help make their respective cases within the Future Force framework. For example, the Royal Navy's Maritime Capability Strategic Vision 2013-2040 focusses on planning 'epochs' and pre-supposes some room for creativity and innovation to be injected into force development. Such an approach could act as a model for a synergising force planning concept that would help drive organic jointness. It could also act as a model for the re-building of the strategic force Britain will need in the twenty-first century if, that is, all three Services can get over the 'not invented here' culture this author has seen too often at close quarters.

Designed to develop Britain's ability to control the maritime and littoral environments the strategy is divided into three 'Epochs' - 2013-2016, 2017-2021, and 2022-2026, and then considers a "Vision Onwards" out to 2040. Epoch 1 harmonises the Navy's efforts with Future Force 2020 with the aim of a Royal Navy able to support a single intervention by 2017, whilst at the same time able to deliver the "standing commitment" of the Royal Navy Command Plan. Epoch 2 aims to have delivered Future Force 2020 and developed the ability of the Navy to concurrently support one simple and one complex intervention by 2020, in addition to a single intervention and the standing commitment. Epoch 3 is focussed on developing sustainability so that stability operations can also be effectively-supported from the sea.

As the Americans also shift to a maritime-centric power projection, the importance of both the strategy and the two aircraft carriers cannot be over-stated. However, there are also very clear constraints, most notably in carrier-operations themselves that will demand innovative solutions. The only allied/partner forces able to 'cross-deck' the Royal Navy's F-35B carrier-based fast jets will be the US Marine Corps and to some extent the Italian and Spanish navies. Given the projected hull lives of these two ships will be out to 2070 it is almost certain that the carriers will need to be converted at some point to fly conventional aircraft, and at significant cost.

The Navy is not alone in facing such challenges which also reflects the dilemma faced by the British as they shift the focus of planning from campaigns to contingencies. Such tension is also reflected in Army 2020 and the attempt to create a well-equipped, properly-trained and fully-funded agile force that can rely heavily on reserves in peacetime. The scale of the challenge is reflected in the cuts to the force laid out in SDSR 2010. The size of the Regular Army has been cut from 102,000 to 82,000, with a new Reserve Army created (replacing the Territorials) of 30,000 part-time soldiers bolstered with additional training and new equipment. Many officers and experts are doubtful that such a reliance on reserves in peacetime is compatible with high-end military operations or even achievable, not least given the nature of the civilian labour market.

The reforms aim to forge a Total Support Concept to better integrate the private sector into forces and operations so that the increasing reliance on reserves can be both realised and realistic. This is vital because if the plan fails so will the Future Force. Indeed, many of the assumptions in SDSR 2010 are based on the support of British business in permitting personnel to take time from their work to serve in the Reserves so that they can train and deploy on operations. It is a big 'if' because for a Peacetime Establishment in a twenty-first century western society such support is by no means a given.

Politically, the need for the Services to continually demonstrate value over cost is vital. In addition to the carriers London now believes other investments in defence equipment may be resumed. The £160 billion of planned investment over ten years is designed to prepare the British armed forces better for future operations given the lessons learned in Iraq, Afghanistan and Libya. These include (*inter alia*) targeting pods for Typhoon fast jets, better protection for Tornado GR4s and enhancements to Merlin helicopters. 13 Squadron Royal Air Force will be re-formed to operate an RAF unmanned Predator capability that is to be doubled, and in 2012 Britain took delivery of its first F-35B Lightning II test aircraft which will be jointly operated by both the Royal Air Force and Royal Navy. Land-based initial operating capability is set for 2018, with initial flights off *HMS Queen Elizabeth* set for the same year.

In that context, "organic jointness" will also be vital to demonstrate value over cost to sceptical politicians and public alike. Central to the Joint Force Concept is a Joint Operating Concept (JOC) and a high-readiness Integrated Joint Force (IJF). Critically, the British armed forces will need to be at the hub of several 'influence relationships', not least to demonstrate their value-for-money. Indeed, one of the primary lessons of the past ten years is that whilst armed forces possess critical planning power such plans are unlikely to be successful if not 'owned' from the outset by key partners – be it other national ministries, state allies and/or partners or civilians critical to campaign and mission success.

The exploitation of knowledge will also be an important change-agent for British forces, with all intelligence embedded to create an organic picture of evolving and real-time risks and threats. London must also better link and exploit lessons-learned from a decade of operational practice to better create a competent, full-spectrum targeting capability and to better exploit data via an enhanced understanding of the mission environment.[124] Equally, this ambition will also require a London much more open to deep civilian access to both military intelligence and planning (which also suggests the need to better exploit unconventional thinking and thinkers).

---

[124] For an in-depth analysis of strategic communications and its role and impact on national strategy see Cornish P, Lindley-French J., and Yorke C. (2011) "Strategic Communications and National Strategy", September 2011 (London: Chatham House).

Getting the force balance right is also an essential challenge in the search for a demonstrable cost-value balance. For example, the Royal Air Force faces a profound dilemma; is it a force committed to a few multi-use types of aircraft, or a force endowed with a lot of aircraft types able to undertake a range of specialised roles? The choice to be made is a critical choice given that the declared roles and missions of the RAF are far more demanding and consuming than today's force can generate; strategic reach, air defence, strike, deployed force protection, and strategic lift.

A further question concerns to what extent, and in what number, Britain should possess certain critical capabilities, such as Unmanned Combat Aerial Vehicles (UCAV) for long-range attack. Or, to what extent Britain should rely on allies to provide them? Is the shift to unmanned platforms strategically, operationally and financially sound? And, of course, what role space - the ultimate global common – and how best to exploit emerging, affordable technologies such as small satellites and reusable launch vehicles for responsive intelligence, surveillance and reconnaissance (ISR)? These are all challenges facing British defence planners as they seek to balance strategic capability and capacity with affordability. Indeed, whilst relying on allies makes good sense politically, it is less so strategically if allies cannot be relied upon to be alongside British forces at the point of contact with danger.

The Nuclear Question

There is also the question of the future nuclear deterrent and its place in British strategy. Britain should retain a nuclear deterrent, but it must be afforded and not come at the expense of a balanced conventional force. In fact, 'the deterrent' has very little to do with British 'strategy' per se. Rather, it is there – an insurance policy - the use of which is hard to imagine. There may be a case for suggesting a limited yield warhead could be used in a counter-force role against the nuclear arsenal of a rogue state, but it is again hard to imagine. There may also be a case for suggesting a British nuclear deterrent could be used in a future strategic nuclear stand-off to create multiple decision-making centres to complicate the calculations of a nuclear peer power. However, that too is at present hard to imagine.

The British nuclear deterrent of today is more a totem of power which only makes sense if the rest of the force reinforces that message through both capability and capacity. The real contemporary issue raised by the deterrent is the distorting effect the cost of replacing Trident will have on the rest of the defence budget. In the past Polaris and Trident were paid for out of the national contingency budget. The decision of the current government to fund the Trident replacement from the defence budget post-2016 will distort defence expenditure further, and acutely so if the defence budget is cut further. This situation is made worse by the inclusion in the defence budget of costs hitherto outside such as pensions and the costs of operations. Indeed, Prime Minister Cameron's commitment at the September 2014 NATO Wales Summit to maintain UK defence expenditure at above the NATO Guideline of 2% GDP looks ever more like an illusion of clever accounting.

The government estimates the cost of the Trident replacement at between £15 and £20bn, whilst some other experts suggest a figure as high as £35bn, albeit spread over many years. £350bn has already been invested to look at the future Trident replacement which, post-Main Gate, will then cost the British defence budget (and not the Treasury contingency reserve) some £100bn over twenty-five years of service. Given the poor record of past big ticket defence procurement projects experience would suggest the latter figure is likely to prove more accurate. Therefore, if the reason for the Trident replacement is as much to do with industry, skills and technology as defence capability surely it should again be paid for out of the national contingency budget?

Britain's Defence-Strategic Partnerships

Broad military coalitions are central to British strategic practice. Operations over (and in) Libya (Operation Unified Protector) demonstrated the importance of a Britain able to generate, at times lead, and act in coalitions that change from operation to operation. Indeed, over Libya some two hundred and sixty aircraft from sixteen

178

states took part flying over sixteen thousand five hundred missions. However, these operations (and subsequent operations over Iraq against ISIS) have also revealed the extent of the shortfalls and weaknesses of both the British armed forces and their European allies that are dangerously undermining both NATO and the EU. As then Secretary of State for Defence Philip Hammond said in October 2012 Libya "shone a bright light on relative military and political capabilities in terms of who 'could but wouldn't' and who 'would but couldn't'".[125]

To help resolve such weaknesses the British must focus on the development of highly-capable expeditionary forces on the premise that the force will normally operate alongside allies and coalition partners. By transforming the British armed force into a highish-end hub or core force would make a major British contribution to a more capable NATO and more strategically-meaningful European relationships, all of which are central to British national strategy. An emphasis must also be placed on capturing and sharing both the lessons and experience gained over many years of operations to exploit the comparative advantage of British military professionals and to thus shape the choices of allies. Much effort must also be made to improve defence and military education, doctrine and training. The trick will be to place the reformed NATO command and control structure at the centre of the British concept of a twenty-first century all-arms force and make effective use of it. This will mean that London must seek to adapt NATO into a much more efficient force-integrator, built on effective strategic mobility together with the resilient and sustainable logistics deployable forces require.

For all the challenges, and if Britain's defence reforms can be made to work Britain's defence model could become the default defence method for all Europeans. Indeed, the defence choices Britain makes are not just about Britain. In a December 2013 conversation at RAF Leeming with a Royal Air Force fighter pilot of 100 Squadron standing next to his aircraft, the problem with Europe's defence was

---

[125] Speech to the RUSI Airpower Conference, Senate House London, 25 October, 2012.

all too clear.[126] At the strategic level there is a growing cultural gap between the British and French, on the one hand, who remain committed to an expeditionary concept of military power, and much of the rest of Europe which is downsizing armed forces in line with Germany's leap of faith into soft power, and the seemingly endless Eurozone debt crisis.

At the operational level the equally toxic effect of over a decade of national caveats and red lines that hampered operational coherence in Afghanistan has sorely undermined trust. The Americans, British, Canadians and/or the French can never be sure that the allies will be with them at the point of contact with danger. Consequently, neither the British nor French are really prepared to step over the sovereignty threshold and abandon a key capability. They both thus maintain at least the appearance of a full spectrum capability, even if for Europe's two residual 'world' powers that means inventories with a little bit of everything, but not much of anything.

At the defence-industrial level the absurd plethora of metal-bashing, basic, defence industries in Europe are kept afloat by narrow, vested interests, the need to keep people employed in the midst of an economic crisis, and a growing interoperability gap between Europeans. The latter gap is now so acute that it is driving deep divergence in the capability choices that Europeans make.

There is however an opportunity that was also apparent from the conversation and concerns how European armed forces exercise and train, and Britain's leadership role therein and thereof. The job of 100 Squadron is to provide "Red Air", i.e. play the enemy so that the latest generation of RAF fighters, such as Typhoon and Lightning 2 (JSF), and indeed those of allies, can preserve a vital war-fighting edge. However, the Hawk aircraft used by 100 Squadron is over 30 years old and whilst good, it will soon be unable to recreate the battle tactics of, say, the latest Chinese and Russian fighters. In a sense, RAF Leeming is fast becoming a Red Teaming hub for British

---

[126] The author visited RAF Leeming to give a briefing to RAF personnel 12-13 December 2013.

and allied forces. However, (and as ever) a good idea is under-funded and thus the effort goes nowhere near far enough.

Ideally, the Operational Training Centre at Leeming should become a showcase for synergy, a place where knowledge, capability, technology and practice come together with synthetic simulation and actual exercising and training. And not just for the Royal Air Force, but also for the Royal Navy and the British Army. To that end, greater knowledge of strategic and operational developments is needed to generate realistic scenarios (something made more pressing by Russia's aggression in Ukraine, China's development of next-generation air combat, a focal point to bring together the best technology for simulation, and the capability to really test military practitioners for the coming challenges.

Such a best-practice centre goal would be at the heart of the Joint Force Concept, itself reinforced by an exercise and training development vision and programme that is in-line with both force and equipment development. If not, the exercising and training capability could soon fall over a relevance cliff, and Britain's armed forces (and by extension those of other Europeans) will only be prepared for what they can do, rather than that which they need to do.

The European angle? There is a vital need to rebuild trust in the wake of the unbalanced campaign in Afghanistan. By turning a base such as RAF Leeming into a European Red Team hub Britain could promote synergy with its own defence strategy and doctrine, and through that, exert political and strategic influence. Critically, value-for-money would be demonstrated, which a politically-savvy MoD must continually seek to do in these austere times. Such an effort would also help restore NATO by emphasising capability, connectivity and co-operative security, the essential tenets of Smart Defence and the Connected Forces Initiative. The good news is that, in setting up the Operational Training Centre at RAF Leeming the Royal Air Force clearly shares at least some of that vision.

Critically, if London really wants to exert defence leverage over coalition partners Britain will need to re-invest significantly in key enabling capabilities because they are the essential assets in coalition operations. Some effort is being made in that direction but as ever far more needs to be done. Britain is revamping its ISTAR, strategic lift and combat air capabilities under the aegis of Future Force 2020. New Atlas and Voyager assets will join the C-17 (strategic air lift), Sentry, Sentinel and Airseeker capabilities (airborne surveillance and command and control) are to be kept, in addition to the increased acquisition of unmanned combat/aerial vehicles that proved effective in Afghanistan.

Specifically, the co-operation over Libya between the RAF and the French Armée de l'Air demonstrated again the importance of the 2010 Franco-British Security and Defence Treaty and the Combined Joint Expeditionary Force (CJEF) concept. The campaign also demonstrated again the importance of bilateral and multilateral interoperability arrangements, which essentially use NATO Standards as the basis for sound force-generation, effective operations and command and control.

With major combat missions in Afghanistan now over it is vital the critical 'corporate memory' of the campaign in captured. The experience British forces have gained must not only be preserved, but built upon to promote force and operational integration with partners forged in campaigns and operations. To that end, work must be extended to maintain the momentum of coalition experience through joint exercises, such as those with the UAE and Oman on Exercise SHAHEEN Star, and with the Five Power Defence Arrangement as part of Exercise BERSAMA LIMA 11 in Malaysia.

GOCO or No Go: A New Partnership with Industry?

Britain's system of defence procurement is a mess and has been for a very long time. The essential problem is that for too long British governments have not been prepared to fund defence equipment acquisition properly. Rather, they have opted repeatedly for short-term options that have put off the real cost of programmes for future governments to deal with. Indeed, London has resorted to a range of ruses as far back as 1998 to avoid this hard reality, and in doing so effectively mortgaged Britain's defence future, which was the challenge SDSR 2010 grappled with. What to do? The 2013 Defence Growth Partnership could at least in theory help to resolve Britain's essential defence-industrial challenge – how to afford the capabilities Britain's armed forces need given Britain's shrinking defence-industrial base and defence budget.

The Government has started to address the challenge, even as ever public pronouncements by ministers have wildly over-stated the progress. On 9 September 2013, Prime Minister David Cameron announced the Defence Growth Partnership (DGP) under the title 'Securing Prosperity – A Strategic Vision for the UK Defence Sector'.[127] Cameron said, "Britain's defence industry is a national success story that we are right to take pride in. Across the country, British engineers, scientists, apprentices and manufacturers are working to ensure that our armed forces have the best equipment in the world. But, as well as making an essential contribution to our national security, industry is vital to economic growth too – with well over 100,000 people employed and a turnover of £22 billion a year. The Defence Growth Partnership sets us and industry a joint challenge to deliver a long-term strategic vision to maintain our position on the leader board – maximising opportunities for British business and further strengthening the economy".[128]

And yet the gap between hyperbole and reality tells a rather different story. On 10 December 2013, the Government abandoned the radical plans for outsourcing defence procurement that had been prepared by former banker Bernard Gray who when appointed to become the Head of Defence Materiel was meant to be the good news message of SDSR 2010. Instead, the existing system was strengthened and run from within government through an agency known as Defence Equipment and Support (DE&S), which is given the money to attract project management talent from the private sector and which Gray heads.

---

[127] See "Securing Prosperity – A Strategic Vision for the UK Defence Sector", https://www.adsgroup..org.uk/pages/02230471.asp
[128] See "Prime Minister Backs the Joint Defence Growth Partnership", 17 September, 2013 https://www.gov.uk/government/news/prime-minister-backs-the-joint-defence-growth-partnership.html

Gray's idea was that responsibility for purchasing defence equipment would be out-sourced to what was dubbed a GOCO – a government-owned, contractor-operated organisation. It was but the latest ruse to get industry to bear both risk and cost for expensive, big-ticket, defence programmes, access private-sector project management expertise (MoD in-house project management 'expertise' is lamentable), and maintain government control. Not surprisingly there were very few private sector takers. Furthermore, the Americans openly expressed concerns that the adoption of GOCOs would lead to the loss of key capabilities vital to future British and coalition military operations by surrendering too many government functions to private contractors.

For all these reasons Britain's 'new' partnership with industry has the look of 'déjà vu all over again'. Genuine collaboration between government and industry will be critical if the unit cost of ever-more complex equipment is to be kept even vaguely affordable and to prevent spiralling defence-cost inflation. Overheads (a euphemism for endless defence-industrial sins) will also need to be kept down, technology pushed-up, and exports sustained to friendly customers the world over. Critical to that aim is an MoD that can genuinely act as an 'intelligent customer' in a partnership with industry that remains committed and honest throughout the acquisition cycle. And, much greater effort will need to be made to exploit commercial, off-the-shelf capabilities and expertise.

The stated aim of DGP is to build upon areas in which Britain is relatively strong, such as air capabilities, intelligent systems and value-chain competitiveness (management speak for effective project management). DGP aims also to develop both the skills-base and international business practice to enable Britain to maintain a major defence and technological industrial base (DTIB). Given Britain's less-than-impressive history of big-ticket defence project management it is a very big challenge.

DGP is also designed to reinforce and exploit the US-UK Defence Trade and Co-operation Treaty which came into force in April 2012. The treaty is designed to assist defence technology transfer between the US and Britain and help industry overcome barriers to such trade, caused mainly by the US International Traffic in Arms Regulations, or ITARS, which have caused significant friction in the past, particularly during the JSF Lightning 2/F35B programme.

For all the challenges Britain still sees itself rightly as an important player in what London hopes will be an emerging transatlantic defence market. However, Britain needs to be careful that its transatlantic ambitions do not fall foul of EU ambitions to create a more coherent European defence market, built on a more integrated European defence and technological industrial base (EDTIB) and of course the imposition of industry-busting regulations by the European Commission. There is clearly some evidence of this in the Commission's stated 2014 plans for an enhanced European Defence Agency, and a single European defence-industrial market.

Speaking at the September 2013 Defence and Security Equipment International (DSEI) conference in London, then Secretary of State for Defence Phillip Hammond warned the European Commission to stay away from any attempt to interfere in defence exports, which he believes should remain national. France, it would appear, agrees with Hammond. In 2013 the Commission launched a new initiative to reform Europe's defence and security sector, and moved Brussels into an area of competence that has traditionally been jealously guarded by the state. The stated aim of the Commission is to lower barriers between national defence markets, help European defence industry become more competitive, encourage synergies between civil and military research, and explore how other areas such as energy, space and dual-use technologies (with civilian and military uses) can contribute to European defence capabilities. However, given the debate over deeper European integration within the Eurozone some will see the timing as linked to Commission efforts to extend its competence at the expense of the member-states, particularly given the Commission's call for Standards that it will both set and control.

Britain's future defence equipment concept emphasises an open architecture that places systems development and integration above platforms. The mantra runs that this approach will be reinforced by the changed relationship between government and defence industries and a new relationship between defence and other industries both in Britain and beyond to exploit skill, knowledge and technologies. All of the above pre-supposes a relatively open transatlantic market.

Certainly, to realise a new balance between a people-centric force and a technology-led force, the relationship with industry will be pivotal. However, the essential challenge will be to retain a sufficiently broad and robust defence and technological industrial base that is also competitive in a world in which many more actors will enter the market, both as defence players and defence equipment producers. That aim in turn will require a very different relationship between the British government and key prime contractors, such as BAE Systems and Thales UK, and an end to the uncertainty caused by over-programming. At the very least, for DGP to have any chance of success, industry will need to be brought earlier into the equipment concept and planning cycle to reduce project uncertainty. Gone are the days when under Smart Procurement a British government could kick the over-priced cost can down the political road by transferring both risk and control to industry. Equally, defence industries (it is hoped) will no longer be able to engineer hidden subsidies by over-charging the British taxpayer.

Changing technology also poses a challenge. For example, the impact of so-called sixth generation (6thG) technologies will also be a factor and the need to incorporate them into existing 4th & 5th generation platforms. Of equal importance will be what not to seek. In other words, part of innovation is the ability to make intelligent choices about what fashion not to follow. At the very least, the British armed forces will need to become more adept at exploiting robust civilian technologies, that may not be militarily bespoke, but which will offer affordable solutions and quickly.

Finally, key capability shortfalls will have to be addressed. Having got rid of MRA4, Britain's strategic airborne eyes and ears are much reduced in spite of Sentinel and Shadow, and none of the fixes to the maritime patrol aircraft (MPA) (such as the use of unmanned aerial vehicles) being suggested by government close that gap. The need is all the more pressing given that a continuously at sea deterrent

(CASD) is dependent on an MPA capability, as shown by the December 2014 incursions by Russian submarines into home waters close to the Faslane base of Britain's deterrent.

Britain and its defence industry also faces a deep dilemma over the balance to be struck between maintaining important strategic relationships, and the extent to which the generations of critical capabilities can be dependent on such relationships. For example, the 2012 debate over a possible merger between BAE Systems and the Franco-German dominated EADS demonstrated, again, that the Franco-British strategic relationship is both important and sensitive. Even though Chancellor Merkel finally killed the prospective deal over the issue of national voting rights and the risk to German jobs, it became increasingly clear that neither Germany nor France were willing to surrender an effective twenty per cent controlling stake in the new company. The deal also suggested a contradiction in London's defence-strategic posture. There seemed little point in such a deal to many with influence in London, at a time of momentous political uncertainty about the future of Europe and Britain's position in it.

Furthermore, (and in spite of the strategic importance of close relations with both France and Germany) with Britain likely to shift to a maritime-centric defence-strategic posture post-2015, and France and Germany essentially remaining continental powers, a profound question arises as to whether in future Britain could meet its defence-industrial requirements under this deal. The impetus seems to have come from EADS Chief Executive Tom Enders and his ambitions to create an aerospace giant that spanned both the civilian and military sectors. The planned parliamentary enquiry into the merger, would almost certainly have found against the merger and that would have made it very hard for the British government to approve the deal in the absence of assurances that neither France nor Germany were in any position (or willing) to give.

The defence-strategic bottom-line is that Britain must be able to fund its Future Force, and industry must be able to supply it. After a decade of failed procurement programmes, such as FRES and

MRA4, and attempts to squeeze too much capability out of limited affordability, reform is vital if defence ends, ways and means are to finally be re-balanced. That will take leadership and consistency. [129] The mantra that the 'unaffordable best' is preferable over the 'good' still tends to dominate British military thinking. Rather, a new type of equipment concept is needed for the Future Force, one that integrates all services, underpinned by a properly-funded defence-industrial concept.

SDSR 2015: The Irreducible Benchmark?

In a September 2014 report by Professor Malcolm Chalmers of RUSI the difficulty of Britain maintaining the 2% GDP commitment made by Prime Minister Cameron at the September 2014 NATO Summit becomes all too clear.[130] Entitled "The Financial Context for the 2015 SDSR: The End of UK Exceptionalism" the report suggests that British defence spending is on track to fall below 2% GDP in financial year 2015/2016 to 1.88%, given that the British economy is growing at or around 3% per annum, and predicted to continue to so do. Current MoD assumptions also suggest that spending will fall to around 1.7% GDP by 2020/21.

However, the current British government is also committed to further spending cuts of possibly up to 25% of public expenditure or £12bn after the May 2015 general elections. Given public pre-election commitments to ring-fence other departmental budgets such as healthcare, education, and aid and development, even the MoD's assumptions, which suggest modest real time growth of 1.2% per annum to the defence budget may prove overly ambitious. Indeed, Chalmers not unreasonably suggests that cuts of between 4% and 10% to the defence budget as part of SDSR 2015 could see defence spending fall as low as 1.5% and 1.6% by 2020/2021.

---

[129] The Future Rapid Effects Systems was a fleet of five Army vehicles with sixteen variants. The MRA4 was designed to be a cutting edge maritime patrol aircraft embedded in the fuselage of a 1950s designed aircraft. Both projects were cut and both have become examples of disastrous procurement practices.

[130] Chalmers, Malcolm (2014) "The Financial Context for the 2015 SDSR: The End of UK Exceptionalism?" RUSI Briefing Paper, September 2014

Set such 'realities' against the rapidly-deteriorating international environment and the challenge faced by London becomes acute. There is every likelihood that not only will Britain be called upon to use its armed forces in the coming years, but that Britain will need forces of sufficient capability and capacity to play a leading role in NATO, EU and coalition operations.

Russia's use of hybrid warfare in Ukraine confirms the need for a twenty-first century NATO concept of collective nuclear and conventional deterrence that includes strategic reassurance and a layered, modernised collective defence built necessarily upon advanced deployable forces, missile defence and cyber-defence. Such a defence would also suggest the need to revisit the old Cold War REFORGER concept whereby US reinforcements were flown in from Continental North America to assist European first-responders. Britain must be at the forefront of such a NATO concept of operations and that will involve forces capable of command, some mass and significant manoeuvre, and a British military capable of leading effective allies effectively.

Furthermore, the campaign against ISIS in the Middle East suggests a new form of super-insurgency that will, in and of itself, demand a British force able to operate at distance as part of a sustained, sustainable super counter-insurgency strategy. Super-insurgencies will operate in the spaces between the emerging great power blocs in the kind of ungoverned spaces which ISIS is successfully exploiting. This is particularly the case in the Middle East where the entire Sykes-Picot state structure is facing collapse, and which is contiguous to Europe. Combatting such super-insurgencies in extremely complicated political environments will thus require a clear understanding that British strategy is designed first and foremost to support the Middle Eastern state in its battle with the anti-state and thereafter to shape the interests and choices of those states. In that context British forces must be sufficiently capable of reinforcing and supporting state partners from the high-end of operations through training and mentoring.

Twenty-first century Britain will also use military power in pursuit of a complex mix of values and interests which merge desired strategic outcomes with humanitarian imperatives. That in turn imposes on Britain's armed forces the need to work effectively, not just across government, but with civilian branches of foreign governments, international institutions such as the UN and EU, as well as different and differing non-governmental communities in international civil society, if influence and effect is to be generated.

Therefore, given the above challenges, SDSR 2015 must necessarily strike a series of balances. Logically, the national level of ambition must remain at least the same as today given the nature of global change. However, even to achieve that limited strategic objective a much tighter relationship will need to be generated by a much meatier National Security Council to promote understanding, planning and action across government. To that end, ministers will need to accept that conflict prevention and deterrence depends in turn on a truly capable British Future Force as the military component of all-important British influence. Such a role is just about afforded by today's armed forces but only just. At the very least recognition of such an influence role would need Government to accept there can be no more military strategic shrinkage given the many dangerous uncertainties that Britain today confronts, and the need to prepare for the consequences of the dangers implied therein.

Therefore, strategically and logically, SDSR 2015 takes places at a pivotal moment at which the strategic assumptions of even SDSR 2010 now seem anachronistic. Or, to put it another way, 2015 will be similar in many ways to 1959 and the end of empire when Britain had to be radical and make some important, radical choices. Back in 1959 the choice was to end conscription, create a professional force and focus fully on the defence of the Euro-Atlantic area. Given the pressures on the United States as it is forced to 'pivot' to Asia-Pacific by the emergence of a robust China, Britain must again make a choice if the centrality of the alliance to an over-pressed America is to pertain.

The British down-payment in Washington for such an alliance demands British investment in powerful armed forces if London is a) to remain an influential voice in Washington; b) help lead European allies back to strategic seriousness via a reformed NATO; and c) reinvest in traditional relationships with Commonwealth powers such as Australia that were long ago abandoned for all-too-short-sighted reasons. In other words Britain can be an important US partner in the emerging American-centric world-wide web of democracies, but only if Britain commits the forces and resources to play such a role.

Given current spending plans and growing strategic commitments striking the right balance will demand of Britain a radical new kind of British force. Hitherto Britain has endeavoured to maintain a 'mini-me' American-style force. SDSR 2015 can no longer sustain such a force given likely spending options and instead will need to pioneer a high-end core force that has significant levels of significant capability but only in return for abandoning some important roles and tasks which it must be assumed will in future become the preserve of allies, either through NATO or the EU. Like it or not, Britain is going to have to specialise.

Given the committed military tasks of the British armed forces SDSR 2015 must address the creation of a deep/organic joint multi-functional force that can act at four levels all of which involve influencing allies, partners, environments and adversaries. Firstly, Britain will need a command force powerful enough to attract allies and partners to organise their own forces in accordance with British force structure. Secondly, Britain must generate a core or integrated force that can act across government and beyond. This will enable Britain to sustain forces and resources during missions at the middle to lower levels of the conflict spectrum such as disaster relief, stabilisation and reconstruction, and consequence management. Thirdly, Britain will need sufficient force to exploit Britain's still residual strategic brand as part of national influence strategies. Influence is not simply a vital component in outreach, but essential to effective conflict prevention. Fourthly, Britain's armed forces must be seen as a flexible core force specifically designed to be reconstituted and expanded should a national emergency emerge. Indeed, the current defence investment programme suggests that just such a force could be created with a bit of imagination. Important new assets and capabilities are being procured which are at present in insufficient numbers to sustain a properly strategic force, but which over time could be enhanced and added to.

However, to realise such a vision when faced by a Treasury and indeed politicians, who will only have eyes for the short-term, Britain's Service Chiefs must prepare and offer a 'radical' value-for-money Future Force plan as part of preparations for SDSR 2015. Critically, such a value-for-money approach will require Britain's Service Chiefs to demonstrate innovation in the application of public money. At one level Chief of the General Staff (head of the British Army) General Sir Nick Carter is surely right when in January 2015, as part of the Army Command Review he moved to cut some one-hundred and fifty of the British Army's five hundred colonels and two hundred brigadiers and generals. It is simply inappropriate and a waste of money for an army that is 25% the size of the US Army to have some 80% of its officers. As Carter said, "It [the senior personnel cuts] will ensure the Army's command structure and its staff are best placed to meet future challenges in an agile, imaginative and effective manner".[131] In an ideal world the cost of funding such posts would be shifted to funding manning and crewing shortfalls at lower levels in the command chain. However, if such cuts are more cuts for cuts sake then they are simply another example of political shenanigans at the expense of the armed forces and Britain's defence.

Britain's armed forces must also become far more 'political'. It is vital that Britain's armed forces take the longer-view, not least to ensure Britain's political leaders do not again sacrifice strategy for politics at the expense of security and defence. Therefore, SDSR 2015 must have a strong vision at its core that considers the horizon out to 2030 and beyond and thus reinforces both the need and the narrative for an organically evolving Future Force. Thus SDSR 2015 must also reinforce the importance of current investment plans as the baseline for a Future Force 2030 (and beyond) and emphasise the need for a period of political consistency.

---

[131] www.itv.com/news/update/2015-01-24/senior-british-army-officers-to-be-cut-by-a-third/

The first order priority is British armed forces conceptually able to think and act strategically. That means the provision of both framework and machinery for strategic thinking that will require a much closer link than hitherto between those that craft national strategy, and those charged with defence and military strategy. This will enable Britain's armed forces to be fully associated with the broad range of security challenges the country faces. However, such a first order priority can only be credible if it is established on a clearly-identified link between national strategy, defence strategy and the scope and size of the force.

Therefore, SDSR 2015 must not simply set the process of organic jointness in train, but must also act as an irreducible benchmark below which the force will not fall. For the Royal Navy the challenge will be to find a reasonable balance between sea control and sea presence. To strike such a balance the future Royal Navy will need more hulls. Equally, the future warship will need to be able to carry out a much wider range of tasks, and work much more closely with land and air forces. For example, during Exercise Joint Warrior your author was surprised that there was no representation from the Army's equivalent of the Rapid Force Task Group – 16 Air Assault Brigade.

The Army is going to have to be ruthless in getting rid of legacy formations and equipment as it shifts from campaigns to contingency, and become far more open to the Royal Navy and Royal Air Force about ways of doing joint business. Army 2020 is already leading in that direction in the consideration of the Adaptive Force, but far more needs to be done. Indeed, too much of the debate, however elegantly made, continues to be about preserving the past rather than preparing for a very different future.

The Royal Air Force must concentrate on air power as the most rapid way Britain can exert strategic influence. To that end, exploitation of technology must be central to the RAF's ethos with a focus on systems rather than platforms. Such a force will emphasise air control, reach and help promote deeper interoperability thus situating the future RAF as both strike force and strategic-enabler. Indeed, critical to the Joint Force will be ISTAR, strategic lift and operational and tactical mobility.

Finally, Future Force 2020 will not be realised. Therefore, SDSR 2015 must reconfigure the effort towards a Future Force 2025 which will have all the necessary components of a strategic force (including a strategic maritime patrol capability). Critical to such a force will be a far deeper level of experimentation and adaption as Britain's armed forces experiment with organic jointness. The bottom-line is this: for Britain's military leaders change is as much about mind-set as military capabilities.

Future Proofing the Future Force

Only through a radical change in the British military mind-set and force structure can a small force serving a powerful state hope to service national strategic objectives in the big strategic space of the twenty-first century. Transforming Defence must therefore mean what it says, rather than become yet another lame attempt by Westminster to present defence cuts as somehow strategic. Indeed, only via strategic unity of effort and purpose can such a Future Force hope to generate the intense interoperability that the Future Operating Environment will demand, and if the British armed forces are to lead coalitions of allies and partners on occasions, and act as a hub for the application of all national means in an emergency.

All Britain's defence-strategic relationships and assumptions will radically change over the next decade and unless Britain's foreign, security and defence structure reflects such change, they will over time decline and fail, and possibly the country with it. To that end, the 2015 Strategic Defence and Security Review must clearly make a statement of ambition that Britain will retain sufficient numbers of world-capable armed forces. If not, all other areas of British strategic influence will be weakened.

Indeed, without such a statement 2015 could well mark the moment when Britain effectively decides it no longer wishes to remain one of the most influential actors, reflective of the world's fifth economy (Britain again overtook France in December 2014), and the third or fourth military-capable power. To realise such ambition Britain must again pioneer (possibly alongside France) an entirely new way of thinking about the relationship between power, influence, armed forces, technology, the society the armed forces serve and, above all, ideas. Much as the British pioneered the modern, professional military force back in the late 1950s, this is one of those moments for profound and epoch-forming choices to be made.

Furthermore, the choices being made by the US, European and new/old partners will also need to be properly considered, as will the defence-strategic and technological choices of potential adversaries and enemies. Specifically, the impact of technology on the structure and strategy of Britain's armed forces will need to be properly thought through. For too long such choices have been driven by urgent operational requirements in Afghanistan, or a cost-driven assessment of how much defence Britain can afford.

Britain's defence planners will also need to think about the unthinkable (and the utterly strategic) given Russia's penchant of late for aggressive behaviour. Humanitarian operations must not become yet another political metaphor for avoiding the dark, dangerous and decisive. Such an analysis would necessarily include *(inter alia)* the impact of new air defences and disruptive technologies, properly unwrap emerging American thinking, such as Air Sea Battle, Global Strike, the Joint Operating and Access (JOAC) Concept and Joint Forcible Entry Operations (JFEO), and their implications for the British order of battle. This effort will necessarily include 6th Generation technologies, area and access denial (A2/AD) and network and cyber requirements, particularly as concerns cross-domain operations and interoperability.

Furthermore, if the British are to invest more political and military capital in the NATO command structure then the Alliance too will need to properly consider such developments. Without such consideration force generation and interoperability will degrade rapidly and NATO's Smart Defence and the Connected Force Initiative will become simply yet more hollowed-out NATO slogans. What is self-evident is the need for deeper partnerships between the British armed forces and beyond, and a recognition that any such partnerships will come at the price of sovereignty and operational flexibility.

The Royal Navy's motto is; if you want peace, prepare for war. Thankfully, Britain today does not have to prepare for war - yet. However, in a world full of friction Britain should at least think about war. And, if Britain is to help prevent conflict injurious to its national interests, all the country's leaders must again learn to think and act strategically. Therefore, SDSR 2015 must finally look beyond Afghanistan and not simply re-fight it. Indeed, the switch from so-called campaigning to contingency operations will make the 2015 review as close to a grand strategic year zero as Britain has known for a century. It is an opportunity to be seized, not squandered.

7.

Little Britain?

"What I set out to do was to virtuously and justly administer the authority given to me. And to do it with wisdom for without wisdom nothing is worthwhile...For each man according to the measure of his intelligence must speak what he can speak and do what he can do"

King Alfred the Great

Re-establishing Strategic Autonomy

Britain must decide what kind of actor it aspires to be in the twenty-first century. The country faces profound strategic choices, none of which are easy and all of which will demand of Britain a strategic renaissance of sorts. Britain still has the capacity and creativity to be an effective strategic security actor. With the world's fifth largest 'real' economy, and pound for pound one of the most capable armed forces across the mission spectrum, the British are still well-placed to exert strategic influence.

However, Britain's cold reality is that the nature of complex change in the world, America's uncertain response to it, European political and military weakness, and Britain's tradition of pragmatic security governance, will continue to place an unforgiving and heavy burden on the British. This book started out by posing a simple question; is Britain and its elite any longer capable of the vision and will required for such influence? In other words, can Britain's elite think big enough and strategically enough about the world for Britain to be a credible twenty-first century security and defence actor? It is a leading and open question with as yet no clear answer.

Britain sits at the nexus between an uncertain American national strategy and pretend European strategy. The consequent vacuum has dangerously-undermined the strategic concept of the West at what is a tipping point in international relations. Strategic leadership is above all about ambition, resources, commitment and consistency reinforced by political vision, rational objectives, effective assessment, relevant and capable structure, and an ability to adjust and re-adjust nimbly in light of events.

With its history, a security policy founded on power and principle, its contacts and its strategic method, its diplomatic style and the quality and capability of its armed forces Britain could still aspire to some form of strategic leadership. Indeed, Britain's genius is the unrivalled ability it has to leverage the power of others through both the legitimacy and credibility of its strategic mission, and the utility of its diplomatic and military means at times of crisis. Given the changes Britain faces it is certainly time to lay to rest the ghost of Suez and, by so doing, re-assert Britain's strategic autonomy from both the United States and the European Union. Paradoxically, both the Americans and Europeans will be strengthened by a Britain that can properly exercise its own national genius for pragmatic strategic leadership.

However, because Britain has abandoned any pretence to strategic leadership, or even autonomy, its major state instruments vital to effective national strategy have become reactive, their efforts divided, and their effectiveness muted. Far from punching above its weight in international affairs, which is a good punch line for a politician, Britain actually punches well beneath it. Indeed, the Foreign and Commonwealth Office (FCO) has become an instrument designed primarily to react to French and German leadership in Europe, and US leadership everywhere else. At the pinnacle of government, the Cabinet Office (and its surrogate the National Security Council) is simply too much of an errand boy, responding to whatever political need the Prime Minister at any given time requires. Indeed, the entire crisis management mechanism focused on COBRA (Cabinet Office Briefing Room A) seems more about appearing to do something when "something must be done", than a system for effective and considered crisis management. Sadly, this means there is little or no effective strategy in London, just politics.

Therefore, Britain must craft and engage a truly British national strategy served by a strategic concept that is properly-funded and founded on a firm belief in the legitimate West as the guarantor of just stability in international relations – a West that is today more global idea than place.

A Turbulent World

British strategic interests are inseparable from those of its partners and allies, but that does not mean Britain must subjugate its interests to them. Unfortunately, the West has lost its strategic way. Therefore, planning must begin now to put the British way of pragmatic security back at the centre of a new Western strategic concept.

Global economic turbulence has traditionally presaged deep global insecurity and instability, and there is nothing in the contemporary strategic runes to suggest that the second decade of the twenty-first century will result in a lessening of international tensions – both within states and between states. Indeed, Russia's aggression in Ukraine demonstrates just how quickly such tension can develop. As a leading European power, Britain will inevitably be called upon to generate more not less security in a big world becoming more dangerous by the day. The main question concerns the extent to which Britain can regenerate a cost-effective national strategy that leads in turn to credible and affordable security and defence, in which all national means will have to be corralled.

For all London's strategic shallowness and its determinedly counter-terrorism, cyber-defence focus National Security Strategy 2010 at least re-opened a debate about Britain's strategic role that had by and large remained dormant for over half a century. Britain's world is not an easy one. The strategic environment is evolving and not for the better. Emerging and re-emerging great power, global reach terror, proliferating destructive technologies, radical belief systems, the increasing imbalance between available energy supplies, rapid fluctuations in the price and apparent availability of fossil fuels, and the seemingly interminable Eurozone crisis are factors driving a new strategic agenda that has been exacerbated by perhaps the worst financial crisis since the Great Depression of the 1930s.

Much was hoped for from the Obama administration, but the President's leadership has been uncertain and his relationship with the British at times cool and distant. This has crucially and critically undermined Britain and the 'Special Relationship' at a vital moment, and thus weakened the central buttress of the transatlantic relationship. Indeed, after a decade in support of the United States, Britain has precious little to show for the sacrifice in Afghanistan and Iraq, other than a loss of status, prestige and influence in both Brussels and Washington. Britain counts for less in Washington today than at any time in the past seventy years.

Britain is particularly vulnerable to what could well be the two headline dangers of the age - renewed and dangerous state competition and the terrifying vulnerability of democratic societies to attack by global reach terrorists and organised crime. For Britain this is a lethal strategic mix as ever smaller, more fanatical groups seek the capabilities to inflict mass destruction and disruption as they gain access to the capital and technologies that at least in principle are afforded them by globalisation. And then there is Vladimir Putin's Russia...

Like it or not, very difficult strategic choices are, and will be, thrust upon Britain that will demand the kind of political leadership and engagement not apparent in London for many a year. The genius of Winston Churchill was not his strategic guidance, which was often very flawed and on occasions disastrous.[132] Rather, Churchill represented the end of an age in which the fashioning of national power into strategic influence taken for granted. This was not just by the fact of British power, but the consensual elite belief that it should be used in pursuit of the national interest. Strategic vision was as much implicit as explicit, and Churchill knew that

---

[132] Perhaps the most tragic example of Churchill's over-reaching grand strategic vision and the distortion of ends, ways and means was the disastrous 1915 Dardanelles campaign during World War One. In his seminal biography of Churchill Roy Jenkins wrote, "Churchill's later summing up was that the concept was overwhelmingly right, that it was only a singularly unfortunate accumulation of narrowly missed chances which prevented it from working...But it is difficult to find a serious military historian who agrees". Jenkins, Roy (2001) "Churchill (London: MacMillan) p 261.

demonstrating an ability to act was as important as the act itself. Constrained as they are by the Human Rights Act and Equality Act, framed by an uncertain and yet defining relationship with the EU, and the consequent weakening of the Special Relationship, London today is a place where power is seen as too often problematic and vulgar, rather than the generator of opportunity. 'Strategy' is thus too often reduced to series of impact studies and risk assessments for fear that national action might offend some group or another.

Trapped between over-reliance on Washington and fearful of home-grown extremists, British strategy is in danger of becoming a form of appeasement, designed to be all things to all men (and women), bereft of direction and passive, leaving a once great country subject to the buffeting of events, rather than shaping them.[133] Britain's retreat into the strategic wilderness is masked by the spin of politics that has too often become the 'stuff' of British strategy. However, sooner rather than later reality must be gripped for the natural consequence of passivity is shock. Possible futures must therefore be considered in the round, not merely used to suggest the government has a grip of the present. Or, indeed, to justify the budget of one ministry against another, which was an essential weakness of both National Security Strategy 2010 and, by extension, Strategic Defence and Security Review 2010.

At the very least, British strategic influence will require engagement on two levels of strategic effect, both of which are dependent upon credible British power and autonomy. At the grand strategic level Britain must devote itself to the re-ordering of stable state relations that recognises the new global balance of state power, which although anchored by the West, will be a world in which neither the US nor the West are dominant. At the regional-strategic level Britain must help engage in the reconstruction of the state in regions such as the Middle East, to prevent state power being 'captured' by non-state

---

[133] Former British Prime Minister Harold MacMillan is reputed to have responded when asked what he feared most by saying "Events, dear boy, events". Reportedly the exchange took place in the early 1960s during a meeting with President Kennedy. However, there is little corroborating evidence and the quotation did not appear in the Oxford Book of Quotations until the 1999 edition.

groups committed to strategic anarchy. With the US focused progressively more on Asia-Pacific that will mean a Britain with sufficient military power to lead Europeans (and others) to help stabilise Europe's turbulent neighbourhood.

Thankfully, for the time-being at least, the question of Scotland's position in the United Kingdom has been resolved by the 2014 referendum on Scottish independence, even if the United Kingdom remains as politically brittle as at any time since its creation in 1707. It may seem strange to some that a book called "Little Britain" did not deal more fully with this issue. However, Scotland's influence must not be over-stated. The country counts for around 8.3% of the British population and 8.9% of the economy with some 60% of the Scottish economy in the public sector. At current rates of economic growth, residual Britain ('Rump UK') would have compensated for the loss of Scotland within five to six years. Moreover, Scotland would have been independent in name only and utterly dependent on the rest of Britain for the massive bulk of its wealth, security and defence.

So, whilst Scotland's future caused uncertainty, its loss would not have greatly materially-affected Britain's strategic position, although it would have certainly complicated key components of Britain's defence, such as the basing of the nuclear deterrent, and would almost certainly have deepened the belief in the High Establishment that Britain had 'had it' and had better accept its fate as simply yet another small EU member-state. Moreover, this book is aimed at the Westminster elite and their failings. Scotland's departure would certainly have strengthened the concerns expressed in this book about London's leadership. The question now is to what extent Scotland's decision to remain part of the UK will lead to a federal Britain, and what if any impact a federal Britain would have on British national strategy. It is a question to which as yet there is no answer.

Britain's Big Strategic Idea

Equally, if Britain is to rebuild itself internally it needs a big strategic idea externally to reinvigorate national strategy and prove the value of a united kingdom. That big idea should be the Liberal Realpolitik – the matching of political determination and the effective organisation of all national capacities and capabilities in the determined pursuit of the value-interest. Above all, Britain needs to craft relevant and effective national strategy underpinned by a cogent, cohesive and convincing national strategic narrative that balances protection of the state with the credible ability to project power and influence. Only then will Britain be in a position to generate and apply all of its still considerable national power in pursuit of a necessarily broad security agenda in a complex and dangerous world. Such ambition, and the crafting of a necessarily ambitious national strategic concept, would in turn require a wholly new approach to British security which should at least be reflected in both National Security Strategy 2015 and Strategic Defence and Security Review 2015, both of which could be important first steps on the road back to strategic influence.

By necessity 'strategy' will involve and require the British to re-establish a distinct strategic identity reinforced by a straightforward, common sense focus on British interests. It will also require the political leadership to say 'no' to assertive Americans, legalistic and/or federalist Europeans, human rights activists, interest groups and exploitative businessmen. At the same time, it will need Britain and its leaders to exert influence over all those states and groups, and indeed beyond. To do that, London's political and bureaucratic elite will need to re-learn the simple facts of national power, its generation, organisation and application. Indeed, in today's environment the security of the British citizen will only be assured through a security policy that is designed from the outset to confront global challenges. For a state that has been by and large focused on Europe for forty years such a shift will require a profound change of outlook, attitude, organisation and, above all, political and strategic mind-set.

Equally, Britain can never hope to lead the West. Rather, British diplomacy should seek state partners the world over with a view to aligning their objectives and methods with British strategy. In one sense, Britain must seek to occupy the vacuum between American grand strategy and European non-strategy. To realise such a goal Britain will need to generate real unity of effort and purpose across government through a National Security Council (NSC) with real political 'nous', chaired by a Security Minister with real political clout.

Only such a radical re-organisation of ends, ways and means implicit in a powerful NSC will an appropriately strategic level of ambition be matched with the resources, instruments and efficiencies needed to secure Britain in a new strategic age. Of course, such a focus on the NSC will doubtless generate the ire of senior civil servants in the Home Office, the Foreign and Commonwealth Office, the Ministry of Defence, and the Department for International Trade and Development (DfID). The Mandarins have long been portrayed as medieval barons engaged in a battle for power and influence within the narrow confines of Whitehall, often at the expense of the national interest, aided and abetted by lightweight political leaders obsessed with the next headline and their own weak grasp on power. This is unfair – well almost. However, over the past fifteen to twenty years or so there has been a steady erosion of coherence and collegiality at the top of government often driven by the parochial ambitions of ministers.

Of course, an effective NSC pre-supposes that lightweight, strategy-free prime ministers would permit a heavyweight security minister to operate to affect – a big if. This is especially so in an age when prime ministers rarely let even foreign secretaries lead on foreign and security policy. And, at the heart of Britain's strategic renovation there must be strategic substance – that means the country's world-renowned armed forces, re-shaped and re-built for a globally-capable role. That will take time and political courage.

In the absence of real national strategy Britain will shift blindly from the regional to the strategic without any rationale for either capability or capacity, and continue to muddle through to exaggerated and unnecessary decline. Not only is the world too dangerous for that, but such a failure of strategy will once again place a disproportionate burden on the young men and women of the British armed forces. They will again be asked to 'make do' in dangerous places often at the expense of their lives. Indeed, in the absence of strategic influence MacMillan's famous dictum about 'events' could well come again to haunt British leaders, as policy is dictated not by Britain, but by the adversaries, enemies, challenges and threats that Britain will undoubtedly face. Indeed, without strategy, the world will seem so much bigger than necessary…and the case for blind dependence on the US, or inevitable marginalisation/subjugation in somebody else's EU, all the more pressing.

A now well-established refrain in London is that in an age of uncertainty one cannot and does not make choices. In fact, an age of uncertainty is precisely the time to make choices, because such choices are vital for the removal of said uncertainty. What such sophistry suggests is that those in London responsible for strategy lack the will and imagination needed to properly reform the great instruments of state, and to prepare them to better face the undoubted challenges that lie ahead.

Given that context, British security and defence policy is facing somewhat of a dilemma. The ends of British security and defence policy can be thus summarised: ensuring a secure and resilient Britain and the shaping of a stable world with the aim of reducing risk and danger to the British people. Such aspiration also drives security and defence strategy which is a function of policy and which in turn is critical to closing the gap between ends, ways and means. For a country such as contemporary Britain this places a particular emphasis on innovation (both civilian and military) if the ends are ever to be realised.

However, innovation is constantly blocked by the self-satisfied belief, and an underlying assumption of British national strategy, that Britain is a status quo power and therefore any change is by definition bad. Not only is this an increasingly questionable assumption that has made Britain reactive, all of Britain's strategic assumptions could well be torn apart over the next decade by the pace, scope and shift of power away from the liberal state towards the illiberal state and non-state. If London continues to wallow in the mud of complacency Britain will become ever more defensive in the face of change – both in Europe or the wider world – and which will most certainly not be in Britain's favour. And, the culture of decline management at the top of government, which has done so much damage to Britain, will continue unabated until a once great country still capable of greatness really does become *Little Britain*.

Professor Paul Cornish has said that strategy must be purposive and that whilst the future cannot be predicted it can at least be shaped, and given sufficient ambition and strategy, crafted.[134] Indeed, he goes on to suggest that strategy is the pursuit of national goals in an increasingly complex and shifting international environment with increasingly limited national resources. Such 'strategy' pre-supposes that British governments are purposive and have strategy goals to match, beyond the maintenance of the current international system of international relations.

If Cornish is right at the very least Britain must generate a British national strategy that properly reflects big thinking about a big future in a big world necessarily well beyond Europe. In other words, it is no longer sufficient for Britain simply to react to the ideas of others – balancing has reached its limits. Britain must once again think and act strategically.

Britain's New Strategic Narrative

British military power has been a central theme in this book and is certainly essential for a coherent national strategy. However, as Clausewitz appreciated diplomatic and political factors are also vital. In all strategy the critical relationship is that between the people and power. Unless the British can restore a sufficiency of social and

---

[134] Professor Paul Cornish, "National Strategy in the Early 21st Century: Innovating for Uncertainty". A paper to the National Institute for Defence Studies, Tokyo, 25-26 October, 2012.

national cohesion, Britain's ability to project influence and power will be severely constrained, and with it Britain's security.

Therefore, Britain is in urgent need of a strategic narrative and only a sound British strategy can provide such a narrative. All states use history to create a sense of patriotism. Indeed, it is the identity of the people with the state that is the essence of the state. Unfortunately, the assault by the political Left on British identity, and the profound ignorance of history by much of the political Right, has further undermined efforts to reinforce Britain's historical narrative with a strategic narrative. The result is that the story of Britain's role in the world is polluted daily by attempts to impose twenty-first century values on eighteenth and nineteenth century actions often as a way to shame the British into inaction. The result is the artificial acceleration of national decline as a consequence of guilt by distant association. The British elite must move decisively to correct the narrative of self-decline because it is undermining any chance Britain may have to prepare properly for the defence of its legitimate future.

Britain's history suggests that whilst misadventure and criminality can be found the British were amongst the most radical of liberal reformers and remain so today. Indeed, it was the merger of British power with Victorian liberalism that led to the creation of much that is good in the world of today. History is always comparative, and comparatively the British contribution to peace, stability and justice has been outstanding. A British strategic narrative must reflect that for without it consensus over British national strategy will be very hard to forge in an increasingly diverse and uncertain society and what is needed is decisive political leadership to that end.

Sadly, the very process of strategy-building has become part of Britain's problem. Strategy in Britain is too often an exercise in bureaucracy and ultimately futility. Indeed, if the National Security Council is to amount to anything leaders must take British national strategy back from the bureaucrats, and Britain's story back from historical revisionists and doom-mongers. In other words, it is not just threats and challenges that must be confronted, but the very culture that the modern British elite have created. Failure to do so and the national cohesion upon which strategy and policy is reliant will be dangerously partial and incomplete. 'Strategic-lite' might perhaps better describe British efforts of late, with too great an effort placed on comforting the wider public, rather than securing them. Moreover, British leaders will need to get a grip quickly if London is to arrest a rapid descent into strategic denial that makes it hard often to discern linkages between political intent and government action.

Therefore, the British need to be very clear about the whys and wherefores of their national strategy because selling it to a sceptical public will prove challenging. The message should be clear; Britain must play a full role in guiding the world safely through profound strategic transition and that the objective of transition must be in the British interest. Too often the implicit message from a London paralysed by political correctness is that Britain is simply keeping the system warm until the likes of Germany, China and India takeover. It is complete and utter nonsense. Britain must compete not pacify.

Successful transition from a British viewpoint will be achieved through the embedding of new power through partnership if possible in functioning institutions central to the system of global security governance that the West created. It will also be achieved by actively reinforcing the legitimate state as the focal point for twenty-first security and identity, even as the old post-colonial order is being torn down across large swathes of the world by radical anti-state elements. That means the British people must support a credible ability and capability to engage in all forms of co-option and coercion because like it or not Britain IS engaged in an existential battle.

The whole question of where best to invest in security will also need to be re-visited if the home base is to be protected given the necessarily complex layers of defence that contemporary security demands. Such security will and must combine effective intelligence, kinetic layers of defence, protection of critical infrastructures and cyber-defence. Security will also require a robust and resilient society sufficiently coherent to understand the risk and willing as a national community not only to pay for its security and defence, but to play an active role in it. Indeed, a secure home base is the *sine qua non* of power projection. And, Britain will need to project power.

Therefore, the successful crafting and execution of effective national strategy in the contemporary age will likely require more than the traditional British High Establishment penchant for incrementalism. There are significant parts of Britain's security and defence architecture that will need to be re-thought if radical Britain is to prepare effectively to confront a radical age. 'Strategic' will need to mean strategic.

Little Britain?

James Harrington once wrote, "No man can be a politician, except he be first a Historian or a Traveller, for except he can see what must be, or what may be, he is no politician...but he that neither knows what has bin, nor what is, can never tell what must be, nor may be".[135] With the December 2014 withdrawal of British combat forces from Afghanistan barring shocks Britain will for the first time in a generation contemplate its place in the world without the backdrop of committed and major military operations. The run-up to National Security Strategy 2015 and Strategic Defence and Security Review 2015 should thus ideally see a profound reassessment of Britain's national interests.

Therefore, this really is a big strategic moment and Britain's little politicians could predictably blow it. Strategic shrinkage, i.e. Britain's reduced capacity to deal with challenges, is a fact and must be addressed. At the very least many of the assumptions concerning Britain's strategic interests must be considered and re-considered in the light of the exceptional change that is taking place in Europe and the wider World.

Equally, strategic planning never takes place in an entirely free space, as Sir Hew Strachan has pointed out.[136] There are always a

---

[135] See Powell, Jonathon (2010) "The New Machiavelli: How to Wield Power in the Modern World" (London: The Bodley Head) p. 55.

host of enduring commitments that must be upheld. As Sir Lawrence Freedman recognised national strategy must also contend with a perpetually moving target. "Strategy is often expected to start with a description of as desired end-state, but in practice there is rarely an orderly movement to goals set in advance. Instead, the process evolves through a series of states, each one not quite what was anticipated or hoped for, requiring a reappraisal and modification of the original strategy, including ultimate objectives".[137] In other words, strategy is, and must be, organic and living.

And yet many of the 'reasons' are in fact little more than poor excuses for inaction. With Britain's future place in the European Union now in doubt and questions as to the future interest of the US in NATO, and indeed in Britain, the strategic choices London makes over the next five to ten years or so could represent the most profound re-orientation of British foreign, security and defence policy since 1945, if not earlier.

The principal aim of British strategy is the same as that of any other leading state - safeguarding the nation, the economy and society. Sadly, the retreat from strategy that has affected and afflicted much of Europe including London, now sees an essentially defeatist and declinist British political class and its supporting Establishment too often seek solace in political clichés that reflect more their own strategic fatigue than fact. In spite of the undoubted change that is taking place in the world London routinely exaggerates the capability and ability of the emerging powers to shape the strategic environment, and under-estimates its own.

There is an alternative British reality and indeed future. The Queen's 2012 Diamond Jubilee celebrations demonstrated both Britain's strength and its weakness. Whilst the vast majority of the British people still believe in Britain as an independent power in the world, many of those at the head of Westminster politics and Whitehall

---

[136] Strachan. H. (2005), "The Lost Meaning of Strategy", *Survival* (Vol. 47, No. 3, Autumn 2005), p. 52
[137] Freedman, Sir Lawrence (2013) "Strategy: A History" (Oxford: Oxford University Press) p. xi

bureaucracy simply do not. Britain's declinist elite is a latter day proponent of Churchill's view about the French in the aftermath of the First World War. "Worn down, doubly decimated, but undisputed masters of the hour, the...nation peered into the future in thankful wonder and haunting dread. Where then was that SECURITY without which all that had been gained seemed valueless, and life itself, even amid the rejoicings of victory, was almost unendurable? The mortal need was Security". Britain's High Establishment must finally begin to stand up for Britain and at least suggest they actually believe in Britain and its people.

There can be no question that with the right will Britain could do far more, even alone, and even with minimal international support were domestic opinion confident that Britain's leaders were up to the task and prepared to accept the costs and sacrifices of action. At the very least, the British could do more to place themselves again at the centre of the 'West'. The alternative is security pretence, isolationism and decline into which much of Europe has already fallen. Self-delusion may be comforting in the short-term, but it is dangerously misguided over the medium to long term.

British strategy must thus have four essential elements:

1. Keep the US engaged in European security and defence by demonstrating to Washington that Britain is prepared to 'lead' Europeans in serious defence investment. This will also help ease American over-stretch by keeping the US strong where it needs to be strong through an equitable sharing of burdens;
2. Establish a Euro-strategic partnership with Germany that recognises Germany's 'strategic' role in European economic and political stability, in return for Berlin recognising British and French leadership of Europe's military effort. France will resent German leadership and further resent any relationship between London and Berlin that might appear to eclipse the Franco-German axis. London will need to work hard to overcome French suspicions;
3. Maintain the Franco-British strategic defence partnership with a particular emphasis on a joint effort by London and

Paris to improve and increase European expeditionary military capabilities; and

4. Re-establish and restore relationships with the English-speaking Commonwealth (Australia, Canada, et al) to reinforce a Congress of Democracies as central to a new West, a world-wide web of secure democracies.

Finally, Britain must urgently re-consider in the round (and properly) policy, strategy, structure, forces and investment if London is to be credible as a shaper, deterrer and actor in the face of coming challenges. Britain's strategic bottom-line is this; if London continues to strip, denude and cut the tools of national strategy simply to placate the politics of the short-term then the costs of the long-term will grow exponentially. Indeed, only by properly investing in effective diplomacy and a powerful military will Britain be able to influence Washington, the EU, NATO and the UN. Britain long ago abandoned its position at the centre of affairs and will thus need to make a concerted strategic effort to re-establish sufficient influence over them so that once again Britain can multiply influence via leverage. Britain faces a choice; invest in the power necessary to achieve both the means and ends of strategy…or face the consequences.

Britain remains a serious if modest power in a world made safer when the democracies are strong. With decent leadership it could again be an influential power. Some ages forgive mediocrity the coming strategic age will be no such age. As Plato once said, only the dead have seen the end of war.[138]

The book started with a quote from General Sir Nick Houghton and it just about finishes with one. "I am convinced that the provision of…security cannot be wished away; and will remain one of the defining duties of government. But the Armed Forces will need to evolve to ensure that they remain appropriate to the demands of the age in which they live. And the country must sustain the appetite to use them appropriately in the national interest".[139]

---

[138] See www.plato-dialogues.org/faq/faq008.htm
[139] "Lecture by General Sir Nicholas Houghton GCB, CBE, ADC Gen, Chief of

Machiavelli once wrote, "All courses of action are risky. So prudence is not in avoiding danger (it is impossible) but calculating risk and acting decisively. Make mistakes of ambition, not mistakes of sloth. Develop the strength to do things, not the strength to suffer". *Little Britain?* Only if Britain's political class continues to talk the talk of power, but in fact walk the walk of irresolution and weakness they have trodden for far too long.

"There is a tide in the affairs of men, Which taken at the flood, leads on to fortune; Omitted, all the voyage of their life Is bound in shallows and in miseries, On such a full sea are we now afloat, And we must take the current when it serves, Or lose our ventures"

William Shakespeare

Julian Lindley-French,
February 21, 2015

---

the Defence Staff, UK Ministry of Defence", Royal United Services Institute, December 18, 2013 http://www.rusi.org/events/past/ref:E5284A3D06EFFD.

Bibliography

Bobbitt, Philip (2002) "The Shield of Achilles: War, Peace and the Course of History" (London: Penguin)

Churchill, Winston (1948) "The Gathering Storm" (London: Houghton Mifflin)

Cohen, J.M. and M.J. (ed.) (1989) "The Penguin Dictionary of Quotations" (London: Omega)

Ferguson, Niall (2004) "How Britain Made the Modern World" (London: Penguin)

Freedman, Lawrence (2013) "Strategy: A History" (Oxford: Oxford University Press)

Gorka, Katharine C. & Sookdheo, Patrick (2013) "Fighting the Ideological War: Winning Strategies from Communism to Islamism" (Washington: Isaac)

Handel, Michael I. (2007) "Masters of War: Classical Strategic Thought" (London: Routledge)

Gray, Colin S. (2005) "Another Bloody Century: Future War" (London: Weidenfeld & Nicholson)

Hastings, Max (2013) "Catastrophe: Europe Goes to War 1914" (London: William Collins)

Herd, Graeme P. & Kriendler John (2013) "Understanding NATO in the 21st Century: Alliance Strategies, Security and Global Governance" (London: Routledge)

Herman, Arthur (2004) "To Rule the Waves: How the British Navy Shaped the Modern World" (London: Hodder & Stoughton)

Howarth, David (2003) "British Sea Power: How Britain Became Sovereign of the Seas" (London: Robinson)

Hurd, Douglas (2010) "Choose Your Weapons: The British Foreign Secretary 200 Years of Argument, Success and Failure". (London: Weidenfeld and Nicholson)

Jenkins, Roy (2002) "Churchill" (London: Pan)

Kampfner, John (2003) "Blair's Wars" (London: Simon & Schuster)

Kaplan, Robert D. (2002) "Warrior Politics: Why Leadership Demands a Pagan Ethos" (New York: Random)

Keegan, John (1993) "A History of Warfare" (London: Pimlico)

Keegan. John (2005) "The Iraq War" (Ottawa: Vantage Canada)

Kennedy, Paul (2004) "The Rise and Fall of British Naval Mastery" (London: Penguin)

Kennedy, Paul (1988) "The Rise and Fall of the Great Powers" (New York: Random House)

Kennedy, Paul (2014), "Engineers of Victory" (London: Penguin)

King, Anthony (2011) "The Transformation of Europe's Armed Forces from the Rhine to Afghanistan", (Cambridge: Cambridge University Press)

Kissinger, Henry (1994) "Diplomacy" (New York: Touchstone)

Lord Moran (2002) "Churchill at War 1940-45" (London: Robinson)

LaFeber, Walter (1991) "America, Russia and the Cold War 1945-1990" (New York: McGraw Hill)

Lawrence, James (2001) "Warrior Race: A History of the British at War" (London: Abacus)

Liddell Hart, Basil (1991 ed.) "Strategy: The Classic Book of Military Strategy" (New York: Meridian)

Lindley-French, Julian (2007) "NATO: The Enduring Alliance" (London: Routledge)

Lindley-French Julian (2008) "A Chronology of European Security and Defence 1945-2007" (Oxford: Oxford University Press)

Lindley-French Julian (2010) "Britain and France: A Dialogue of Decline?" (London: Chatham House)

Lindley-French Julian and Boyer Yves (2012) "The Oxford Handbook of War (Oxford: Oxford University Press)

McCardle Kelleher, Catherine & Reppy, Judith (2013) "Getting to Zero: The Path to Nuclear Disarmament" (Stanford: Stanford University Press)

McKenzie Mary, M. & Loedel, Peter H. (1998) "The Promise and Reality of European Security Co-operation: States, Interests and Institutions". (Westport: Praeger)

McNamara, Robert (1990) "Out of the Cold: New Thinking for American Foreign and Defence Policy in the 21st Century" (London: Bloomsbury)

Meyer, Christopher (2003) "DC Confidential" (London: Weidenfeld and Nicholson)

Paxman, Jeremy (1990) "Friends in High Places: Who Runs Britain". (London: Michael Joseph)

Powell, Jonathan (2010) "The New Machiavelli: How to Wield Power in the Modern World" (London: The Bodley Head)

Rapaport, Anatol (ed.) (1968) "Carl von Clausewitz: On War" (London: Penguin)

United States Institute for Peace and the United States Army Peacekeeping and Stability Operations Institute, (2010) "Guiding Principles for Stabilization and Reconstruction" (Washington: USIP/PKSOI)

Smith, General Sir Rupert (2003) "The Utility of Force: The Art of War in the Modern World" (London: Allen Lane)

Tuck, R. (1991) "Hobbes Leviathan" (Cambridge: Cambridge University Press)

Van Crefeld, Martin (2000) "The Art of War: War and Military Thought" (London: Cassell)

Reports

"A Strong Britain in an Age of Uncertainty: The National Security Strategy" (London: HMSO)

Chalmers, M (2014) "The Financial Context for the 2015 SDSR: The End of UK Exceptionalism?" (London: RUSI)

Cornish P, Lindley-French J., and Yorke C. (2011) "Strategic Communications and National Strategy", September 2011 (London: Chatham House).

"From St Malo to Nice – European Defence Core Documents" (2001) (Paris: WEU ISS)

"Securing Britain in an Age of Uncertainty: The Strategic Defence and Security Review 2010" (October 2010) (London: HMSO)

"The National Security Strategy of Japan", (2013) (Tokyo: Japanese Government)

"The National Security Strategy of the United Kingdom: Security in an Interdependent World" (London: HMSO)

"The Strategic Defence Review and the National Security Strategy – Sixth Report of Session 2010-2012". House of Commons Defence Committee (2011) (London: HMSO).

42028923R00124

Made in the USA
Charleston, SC
15 May 2015